Praise for *36 Islands*

'A *Swallows and Amazons* adventure for the modern day by one of the most interesting travel writers working today: *36 Islands* is a journey to the forgotten parts of the Lake District that weaves together philosophy, psychology, poetry, literature, folklore, angry swans and damp pot noodles, and reminds us of the healing power of the forgotten wildernesses close by us' Dr Bijan Omrani, author of *Caesar's Footprints*

'A headlong plunge into the deep, dark waters of the Lake District and its islands. Packed with curious historical facts, philosophical and literary footnotes and a highly entertaining sense that every other visitor to the Lakes is an interloper, you can feel the chill of waters creeping into your bones as Twigger paddles his way to some of the most inaccessible spots of this liminal hinterland. I really enjoyed it'
Shaun Bythell, author of *Diary of a Bookseller*

'Twigger has an inexhaustible curiosity, a childlike desire to explore and bags of energy . . . the author is full of stories . . . He visits all the well-known lakes (and some not – who has heard of Devoke Water?), exploring islands that inspired Beatrix Potter and William Golding, as well as the ever-present Ransome. It's usually raining, but he's an irrepressible optimist . . . The world is a better place with adventurers such as Mr Twigger about' *Country Life*

'Into his charming, pottering narrative Twigger braids an account of the eccentric Ransome and his reason for creating the world of *Swallows and Amazons* . . . Twigger intersperses his narrative with a series of hand-drawn maps, giving the book a wonderfully homespun feel'   *Mail on Sunday*

'Terrific . . . In the past, Twigger has written acclaimed travelogues about the Himalayas, the Rocky Mountains and the Sahara. With *36 Islands*, he brings the same wide-ranging curiosity and intelligence to bear as he walks, paddles and kayaks through some of Britain's most stunning, and sometimes still unspoiled, scenery . . . we learn a lot about Ransome too'   *Reader's Digest*

'There is something both comical and Zen like about Twigger's work, and everyone is the better for it'
     The Scotsman, Best Books of 2022

'Armed only with an inflatable canoe, Twigger – a man resolutely fascinated by uninhabited isles – journeys beyond the tourists and busy roads to explore Cumbria's finest. In doing so, he visits both real and remembered islands, drawing inspiration from the Lakeland poets, Alfred Wainwright and others, to redraw his own map of the Lakes and visit a place very different to the one we know'
     Wanderlust, Best Travel Books of 2022

36 ISLANDS

In Search of the Hidden Wonders of the Lake District and a Few Other Things Too

ROBERT TWIGGER

WEIDENFELD & NICOLSON

First published in Great Britain in 2022 by Weidenfeld & Nicolson,
This paperback edition first published in Great Britain in 2023
by Weidenfeld & Nicolson
an imprint of The Orion Publishing Group Ltd
Carmelite House, 50 Victoria Embankment
London EC4Y 0DZ

An Hachette UK Company

3 5 7 9 10 8 6 4

A CIP catalogue record for this book is
available from the British Library.

ISBN (Mass Market Paperback) 978 1 4746 2163 2
ISBN (eBook) 978 1 4746 2164 9
ISBN (Audio) 978 1 4746 2165 6

Typeset by Input Data Services, Somerset

Printed in Great Britain by Clays Ltd, Elcograf S.p.A.

MIX
Paper from
responsible sources
FSC® C104740

www.weidenfeldandnicolson.co.uk
www.orionbooks.co.uk

To Justin Rushbrooke
amicus verus est

Contents

The Lakes

Haweswater

Ullswater

Windermere

Coniston

Devoke Water

Derwent Water

Ennerdale

Loweswater

Crummock Water

Thirlmere

Grasmere

Rydal Water

Elterwater

The Islands

Wood Howe

Norfolk Island

Cherry Holm

Wall Holm

Lingy Holm

Kalila

Dimna

Bee Holme

Belle Isle

Crag Holme

Crow Holme

The Lilies

Lady Holme

Ramp Holme

Maiden Holme

Rough Holme

Peel Island

Watness Coy

Lord's Island

St Herbert's Island

Smoke Island

Derwent Island

Norway Island

Invisible Island

Gaffer Tape Island

Blue

Deergarth

Hawes Howe

Scarehorse House Island

Oak Island

Magners Isle

Stairway to Heaven Island

Crusoe Island

Dogowood Island

Silver Holme

Blake Holme

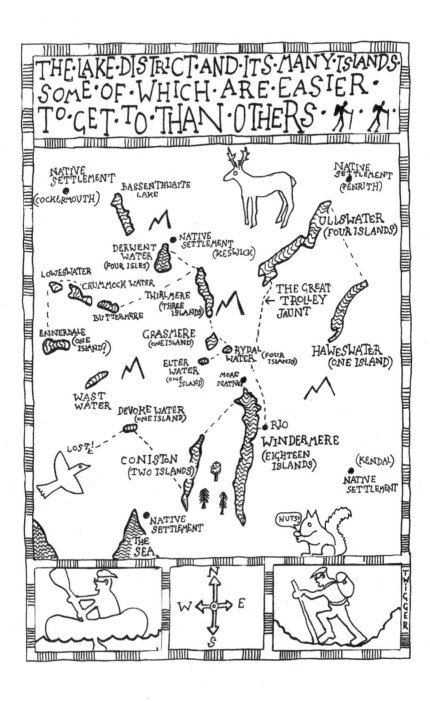

ONE

On Approaching Uninhabited Islands

The garden was dry and sandy, with Scots pines and a view of the sea. An odd sort of rock circle within the trees was a 'Roman camp', my cousin told me. Every day was some kind of adventure: digging quartz crystals out of the cliff, descending into sea caves, capsizing in a tiny blow-up rubber raft. In the evenings, my father read to us before bed, something he only did on holiday as all of us could now read ourselves. I was seven years old, my sisters nine and five. The book he was reading was *Swallows and Amazons*. I was used to Enid Blyton; this book was different and much more realistic though ostensibly the same genre: four or five kids have a big adventure and outwit the adults along the way. But in this book, by a man called Arthur Ransome, the children had skills and they knew things I didn't, things like sailing and rowing and lighting fires. This book opened up an entire world of competence I had only dimly perceived before. A whole world of freedom to go places alone, without adults, to the most exciting sort of places . . . islands.

Who doesn't have a thing about islands? From Arthur Ransome and Enid Blyton via *Robinson Crusoe* (Defoe's original as well as the 1960s Franco-German TV series starring Robert

Hoffmann), *Lord of the Flies*, *Mutiny on the Bounty*, not to mention Tracy Island in *Thunderbirds* and, later, *Papillon*, *Cast Away* and even that Bear Grylls series where regular folk tried to be desert island survivors. Islands are just the best and most concentrated form that adventure can take – as long as they are small enough and uninhabited enough.

And the Lake District is full of small islands. Islands that I ended up thinking about in forty years of visiting the place while never *once* setting foot on one. By 2021, I had done my share of Wainwrights and obscure fells, I had camped and climbed certain classic rock routes. I'd spent New Year's Eve getting lost in a snowstorm on Sty Head pass, but I'd never swum, paddled or sailed to one of the thirty-six islands in the Lake District.

So the mission was simple: visit these thirty-six islands before it got too cold and miserable or another lockdown happened. I had in my mind a plan to camp on quite a few, which I knew even without checking was strictly *verboten*. Going in the summer and autumn would provide the best chance of good leaf cover; a bare winter island is a bad place to hide out on.

Which brings me to the next thing, the subtext of the whole escapade. On the surface I was travelling about admiring the many islands of the Lake District, noting birds and nature and other such fine things. But beneath the surface, in the liminal zone where the low tide of the unconscious reveals itself through the strange flotsam that it leaves on the shore, where urges are given incomplete explanations, there, I was on a mission to find a potential bolthole come the next disaster after Covid. Possibly a nuclear exchange courtesy of a misunderstanding in western Ukraine? I didn't know.

But the unconscious knew; it knew that a deserted island in the middle of a lake, possibly full of fish, might well be a good place to hunker down while the apocalypse played out. So, on the one hand it was about a jolly jaunt around the summer isles of Cumbria, while on the other Mr Hyde was looking for a bucolic bunker to hide away in. Escape. Which I have been doing for most of my adult life in one form or another, just not from anything as potentially disastrous as a societal meltdown.

I'm a travel writer who has mainly written about journeying abroad. But my last book, *Walking the Great North Line*, took me up a dead straight route from the south coast to Northumberland, through forty or more ancient sites. I'd walked the whole way and learnt: a) most of England consists of green fields with nothing in them; b) people are 98 per cent friendly; c) stealth camping is stressful unless you have a buddy; d) there are still discoveries to be made; e) incongruity and weirdness are everywhere, including where you least expect to find them; f) our preferences don't really change, but the reasons and alibis we provide do; and, g) Derbyshire is the banter capital of the UK.

I was quite late in singling out these particular islands for special attention; Wordsworth in his excellent and still pertinent *Guide to the Lakes* of 1835 wrote: 'The lakes had now become celebrated; visitors flocked hither from all parts of England; the fancies of some were so smitten that they became settlers; and the islands of Derwentwater and Winandermere, as they offered the strongest temptation, were the first places seized upon, and were instantly *defaced* by the intrusion.'

How you manage the tourists – *the defacers* (excluding oneself in such considerations, of course) – in your head as much as on the narrow C-roads and in the carpark, is important. In Arthur Ransome's books they are simply redesignated 'natives' and ignored, made invisible as natives were made invisible throughout the British Empire (though Arthur is in no way a conventional imperialist). It was a masterstroke that returned the Lake District to its true role: a backdrop to whatever fantasy we should choose to project upon it.

So important mission manuals or guidebooks for me would naturally include Ransome's Lake District books for children, especially *Swallows and Amazons*, which is the one with the most islands in, including Wild Cat Island, the place I most wanted to visit; a place that occupied for me, I felt, the same emotional location that a much loved movie or pop star does for people who grew up fantasising about films and music, which I didn't.

After all, who could ever forget, once read, the famous telegram that kicks off *Swallows and Amazons*? I'd even used it as a guide for bringing my own kids up (with inconclusive results): 'BETTER DROWNED THAN DUFFERS IF NOT DUFFERS WONT DROWN.'

But now I was really going to go there, certain thoughts crowded in: did I need a wetsuit? And what kind, if any, of buoyancy aid? And was I, heaven forbid, perhaps a duffer who might drown? I had made long trips by canoe in Canada, but that was years ago. And I had always been especially cautious about lake paddling, having read a sufficiently large number of accounts of people who had drowned when trying to swim the distance from their capsized boats to dry land. Ransome's best friend from school died after just such an incident on

Lake Windermere, in a boat Ransome had advised him to buy . . .

I would start and finish with the islands, with their undeniable allure and endless metaphorical potential. Bound up with islands is the life of Arthur Ransome, the subject of three major biographies, the best two being Hugh Brogan's *The Life of Arthur Ransome* and Roland Chambers' *The Last Englishman*. Chambers has the advantage of never having loved Arthur as a minor god, a mentor, as I did and Brogan evidently did too. Brogan's can be read as a loving indictment of Ransome as a charming man, a narcissist, and a man who never really grew up.* I recognise the Ransome I loved so much when I read the books, but I see his faults too. But on reading Chambers, you realise he was also a rather silly man and your tolerance turns to derision. In other words, you begin to rebel against your first teacher, mentor, father.

When you write a book it's good to have some unresolved and real questions you want to answer hanging over you as a sort of motor to keep you going. This can't be the main question posed by the book, to which you usually already know the answer (hence gaining the confidence of publishers, etc.). The object is not to find an argument to support one side

---

* One characteristic of the narcissist is the nursing of a grievance. And for Arthur that grievance turned around the 'theft' of his library by his ex-wife. For Arthur really isn't a scholar, someone who can use any public or institutional library as if it were his own; he is a childlike collector of books. I had seen this in others and their desire for books as objects, talismanic rather than functional, status symbols for those who doubt their own intellectual prowess but have observed and admired people who have such prowess. A library is seen as the tool they too need, the bit of kit that will win them the same attention. Ransome is very unlike the simple characters he portrays in his books . . .

or the other, which is what you do when you have already
decided something, but instead to genuinely meander and
mosey about, trying to get a perspective, a good look at the
question. When you've had a long enough look the answer
is usually obvious.*

One thing I decided to ponder upon was the notion of
reaching a fork in the path of life. When and where do we
meet them? Why are some irreversible (or seemingly so)
and others mere happy diversions before we are back on the
main route again?

One fork we encounter in middle age is the decision to
either be more open and tolerant of others, or more closed
and set in our ways. Put so baldly, it seems bleeding obvious
that option one is the only choice. But it isn't that simple.
In the following book I hope to explain to myself why some
don't choose it and also how the fork is more like ivy or some
kind of deciduous creeper that keeps coming back; that you
have to keep clearing it away, it's not like chopping down a
tree, and it is the nature of the fork and its gritty everyday
tenacious reality that makes it much harder to deal with than
the theory suggests.

Another question, not really related at all to that of the
forks in life, but one that seems to hover above the writing
of *Swallows and Amazons* itself, is just how much of a pirate
can we be in modern life? The billionaire founder of the
Oracle software company, Larry Ellison, uses 'being a pirate'
as an existential prod in his business life and indeed enjoins
his employees to be piratical too. Having been involved in

---

* Perhaps mirroring the old adage that any problem is easily solved if it is
defined clearly enough.

corporate training with that company, I can safely say piracy is pretty thin among the executive ranks that I encountered, who seem more interested in pay, promotion and early retirement than rum, gold and adventure on the high seas. However, anyone who sided with Nancy Blackett against staid Cap'n John in *Swallows and Amazons* must still have a lingering desire to be a bit of a pirate from time to time.[*] The question is, how much and when?

One of my best Lake District experiences was a family holiday when I was eighteen. We stayed at Loweswater, one of the less frequently visited lakes in the western side of the area. We rowed around the lake in an old boat and even landed on the lake's one micro-island, which was very close to the shore. Yet when I looked at the detailed OS map I couldn't see this island. Had I imagined the whole endeavour? Maybe we'd just landed on the far shore and it had *felt* like landing on an island to me, who had yet to become a connoisseur of island landing.

It seemed to me a further interesting angle of exploration involved looking at how we approach uninhabited islands. I don't just mean the methodology, I mean the whole psychological experience. Approaching an inhabited island is one thing – you bring a whole boatload of presuppositions and received opinions with you, bulky as a hogshead of rum and a bundle of oakum. But what of the uninhabited islands, what resources do you have then? Or perhaps I just mean *unvisited* islands, the ones that we know nothing about. Until we land there.

---

[*] You have to hand it to Ransome in giving the pirate roles to women – not just Nancy and Peggy, but also, later, Missee Lee in the tenth book in the series.

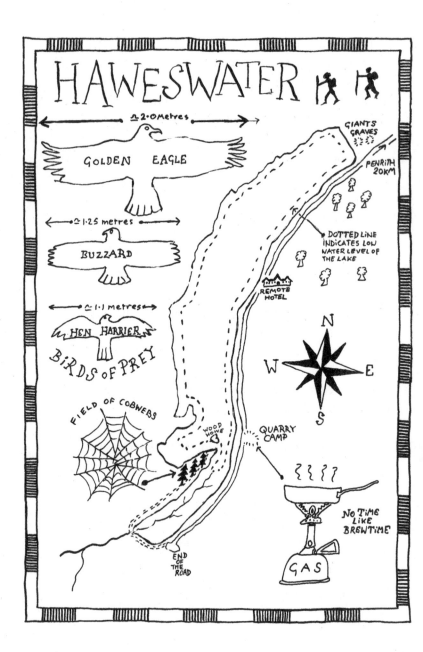

TWO

How It's Done

Lake: Haweswater, 57 metres deep, 6.7 kilometres long,
3.91 square kilometres.
Island: Wood Howe

I typed the lake's name and left it there as inspiration.
Haweswater, maybe because of its homophone 'whore's
water', or maybe because it has a buried tragedy in its past,
or rather a flooded tragedy, well, the name alone seems to
ring out and have its own special resonance in a way that the
names of Windermere and Elterwater don't.

There were good reasons for starting here, both the
journey and now the writing about the journey, after a long
season of doubts and fitful sleeps and illnesses and deaths
and flooding and high winds – all things you might expect
in a region of lakes and mountains, but still I wasn't that
ready for it. But if there is one thing I have learnt, it is this:
there's never a perfect time. Never a perfect time to start, set
off, begin or depart, return, come home, settle in. The notion
of the perfect time and the perfect place and the perfect
pal or perfect husband or perfect wife are all terrible dead
weights that everyone must learn to jettison before they even

attempt to rise on the delicate thermal currents of upper air that are there to help all of us, if we only learn to feel the lightest of breezes. I faffed around with titles and chapters and discovered Ransome wrote twelve books in the Swallows and Amazons series – and that there are twelve lakes with islands in the Lake District and I had roughed out twelve chapters. Good omens!

DROWNED

Back to the start. The heart of it:

> BETTER DROWNED THAN DUFFERS IF NOT
> DUFFERS WONT DROWN.

Faithfully rendered in caps in proper telegram style, this was a message from the children's navy captain father (who we never meet) in *Swallows and Amazons*. The four Walker children are impatiently awaiting permission to camp on the island in the lake. If they can't go to the island the holiday will be spoilt – that's obvious. The children range in age from seven to twelve. Any child who can conceive of such an adventure should be trusted, should be given permission. Only children who inherit adventures, who are along for the ride, should be given a short rein. They haven't earnt it.

But will the Walker children's dad allow unsupervised sailing and swimming, even in the 1930s? When the cryptic (well, not that cryptic) answer comes, the youngest, Roger, doesn't get it. 'I think it means yes,' says Titty (and we'll get to her name later). So they set out – and thus begins one of the greatest series of children's novels ever written.

And it all starts with the desire to camp on an island.

Gosh, now we're really rushing, and I have so much to say too about Robinson Crusoe and the book of the Islamic philosopher Ibn Tufail that inspired it or at least preceded it, about island literature in general and so on and so forth. But already I can feel myself heading towards the idea of off-grid escape that I mentioned earlier.

In my off-grid fantasy, before I even knew much about Haweswater, I had in mind a wooded ravine of water ringed by conifers and a high chain-link fence I'd need to climb to get in. I'd do it at night, so that the driver of the occasional utilities company pick-up that crunched along the gravel access roads would not see me. I would swim to the island, maybe wearing a black wetsuit and towing a black inflatable with my gear inside it. The weather was always warm, clement. There was no hint of rain or high wind – the usual backdrop of the great outdoors.

The good weather, in Britain, is like a half-term holiday: welcome, looked forward to and over all too quickly. You're always 'lucky with the weather' when it's sunny. When it rains a bit, is cloudy and a bit chilly, you're not unlucky – it's just what is expected. And walking in cold weather *is* pleasant. When it's too hot you get sweaty and need to rehydrate all the time. But visiting islands by canoe or sailing boat or rubber raft and dipping your hands in the cooling water, and drinking that water, and splashing around in it on the sandy beach – well, it can never be too warm for that. So in my fantasy it was always warm, clement.

Anyway, given this image of escape, Haweswater had to

be the first place I visited. It's one of the more remote lakes, which was dammed and given an extra ninety-five feet* of depth after 1929 (the reservoir was full by the mid-1930s). In length, it grew from two miles to three and a half. It is strongly walled along the single C-road that runs its length and there is wire on top of the wall. United Utilities signs warn against swimming, camping and any form of ingress other than via the single bridle path on the opposite bank.

It is a steep-sided lake, where forty-five-degree slopes of gravel and rock dip into the very deep and cold-looking stripe of water. Conifer woods surround much of it, so dense they topple over onto the slopes that are left behind when the reservoir runs low. The toppling, commercially planted trees are like shark teeth – expendable, constantly being pushed forward, replaced, eating away at the lake's edge, which is being eroded by the water going up and down. The very nature of its being a reservoir, with its cyclical emptying and filling, brings a hidden aggression to the lake, an omnivorous quality; it becomes like all extractive enterprises: ugly on some profound level, a case of aggression caged by necessity . . . What should be a beautiful shoreline isn't; these are less beaches than 'tide marks', as Wainwright puts it so very well. Pink and grey and beige, these are the recording strata of extraction and replenishment.

At the south end is Wood Howe, a fine wooded island.

In the process of making Haweswater into a reservoir

---

* Sometimes imperial measures are used in this book and sometimes metric. This is intentional. As a child growing up in the 1970s I had to learn both. It was a confusing time – half facing forwards, half mourning the past – and this division continues to haunt me. And, after all, why should it always be either/or?

for Manchester (and currently it still supplies 25 per cent of the population of the North West), a hamlet and the village of Mardale were drowned, including the church and graveyard – the bodies all dug up and moved to nearby Shap. The church tower and all the other village buildings were knocked down and some of the stone used in making the dam, a new kind with many buttresses. But they left the dry stone walls of the fields, which you can see when the reservoir is low, as it was on all my visits to the place.

I had read in W.G. Collingwood's book *The Lake Counties* that 'at Mardale you can see the old Lake District with few modern improvements. Indeed it is less populous than formerly; several houses, once inhabited have fallen into ruins, for nowadays the little farm, which just supported a family of the old type, does not pay. . .'* Perhaps it was this decline (temporary, of course – a house in Mardale, if it still existed, would now go for half a million pounds) that tempted the Manchester Corporation to level the place. Collingwood adds in the 1932 edition of his book, 'it is certain that the damage is done and cannot be undone, though at present the work is in abeyance.' He was wrong: the dam was filled and working by the end of the decade.

Collingwood had been the nineteenth-century polymath John Ruskin's secretary. He was an artist, author and father to the philosopher R.G. Collingwood, whose work I first came across by chance in the PPE reading room at Oxford, probably after a nap (libraries always send me to sleep) – a

---

* As we'll discover, Collingwood was the polymathic author who encouraged Ransome to be a writer. Arthur asked *both* his daughters for their hands in marriage. Both refused.

philosopher who made the simple but very clever observation that instead of focusing on any statement someone makes, we should backtrack to the question *presupposed* by that statement. What is the unasked question they are attempting to answer? And this idea has remained with me all my life (unlike the theories of Hobbes and Locke that I had to bone up on for finals).* You've seen me using it already in these pages. So by some curious alchemy, by finding by *complete chance* an author who was intimately connected to the major influence of my younger years, I was experiencing some kind of destiny, or perhaps had entered an alternative universe and was now living a vicarious rerun of Ransome's own life!

I'll leave that thought hanging for a moment, but let's return to the Collingwood family, who were hugely important to Arthur Ransome (including Robin and the daughters of W.G.); indeed, he claimed he would never have been a writer but for meeting W.G. Collingwood by chance in the Lake District when he was nineteen. Knowing Collingwood changed his life completely.

And he changed mine too, in my own humble way, because if I had not been asleep in the library and woken in a blurry, half-bored way and reached out for a random book on a shelf, I would never have discovered his son R.G. Collingwood (who is now much better known as a historian of Roman Britain, despite being the Waynflete Professor of Metaphysical Philosophy). I would not have then embarked on a mammoth reading of all of his works, which resulted

---

* Major players in the Political Theory papers that I managed to disgrace myself in.

in my agreeing to give a talk on the subject to a nascent philosophical society in Oxford, on which I reneged owing to a perceived insult not even directed at me but a friend, which caused a fellow student not to talk to me for three decades. But then, oddly enough, thirty years on, the same fellow student forgave me for failing to turn up at the allotted time at his society and now we are on pretty good terms. And a person you have angered who then forgives you is a solid friend. A fork had been retrieved!

So the Collingwood magic was there, albeit in diluted form. And since Ransome was so instrumental in igniting my love of the Lake District, and since the Collingwood grandchildren were the models for the children in *Swallows and Amazons*, I was keen to nourish any other Collingwood connections I could find.

DAMMED

Although an ideal example of somewhere untouristy and utilitarian and a bit edgelandish, Haweswater reservoir was also, I had to face it, a tad ugly. I could see all this now as I looked down on it. The water was low: too many thirsty people in Manchester and not enough rain. The revealed land had the mud-slapped, drear look of flood damage. With dry stone walls.

Why did they leave the walls and not the buildings? Why did they have to unleash their violence on destroying the church and its tower? Unburying the dead – well, I understand that. People want to visit the graves of their ancestors. But knocking down, systematically, all the old buildings? The stone, they said, would be used for the dam, and much of it was. But why leave the walls?

After several visits to Haweswater I started to think the idea of destroying every remnant of the village's human existence, its dwellings, was part of the programme of erasure of which the dam was just one small example. The city of Manchester needed water, so take it from the hills, the pristine wilderness. It was a challenge, too; the heyday of damming was in the twentieth century, just as it was the heyday of massive wars of destruction. Damming is an aggressive act. A small dam is a micro-aggression, easy to live with. But a big dam causes problems. Yes, I have an odd relationship with dams.

They seem to me to be harbingers not of life, but of anti-life, doom, gloom, silence, dripping death. I don't quite know why. Is it all that power tied up behind a manmade wall? Is it the potential for utter destruction both created by and put on hold by hubristic man? If a nuclear bomb is a weapon of mass destruction, a dam is an artefact of potential mass destruction. Ah yes, the Dam Busters – look at the damage they caused. The footage of a blown dam, the sheer unbelievable forces of nature unleashed by millions of gallons of suddenly freed water . . . well, go on YouTube and have a look. It's mind-numbing.

A dam is like a bunker for water. And a bunker is where you hide from disaster.

I was looking for an island that would serve the same purpose.

Back to the walls. They loomed up out of the receding mud, worn down and silted up. The walls remained because presumably there was enough stone for the dam in the levelled buildings (though much material was brought in too). They serve to remind us of the fields that are now underwater. Fields can be empty, they don't imply human content or involvement. Or history, really. If you want to erase history, you tear down the homes of human beings.

When the dam was built, shortly after the First World War, history – which had led inexorably up to that war – simply didn't make sense anymore. I mean the Western project of history as a movement towards greater enlightenment and greater good sense. Either you made sense of the First World War as a last-ditch battle against the evil tribe called Hun, or you viewed it as a catastrophic losing of the plot. Either way, history needed to be erased, and what better way than by building new towns, dams, motorways and aerodromes?

Imagine a church tower peeking above the lake's surface whenever the water level dropped, like it did now. How intriguing that would be, but also how messy. Maybe people would want to dive and explore the old houses. Underwater urbex. They'd also be reminded, constantly, of the crime that was being committed to make the reservoir. That a village was destroyed by a private act of parliament to supply water to a giant city far away.

Without modern methods it's harder to erase history. People have tried in the past. Genghis Khan destroyed Balkh and the intricate underground water supply system on which the city was able to thrive. The system has never been rebuilt and Balkh has remained a shadow of its former self ever since. But the ruins, according to the fourteenth-century scholar and explorer Ibn Battuta, were so strongly made they gave the illusion of being inhabited. Muhammad Ali, ruler of Egypt in the early nineteenth century, was famously only persuaded *not* to deconstruct the pyramids because it would cost more than transporting stone from riverside quarries. Oh, and he was building a dam at the time too – the first across the Nile at the head of the delta.

People have always wanted to destroy the past to make their mark on the future. Knock down monuments to build something better – perhaps in the form of a functional monument called a dam. But dams are not like pyramids and castles and old forts: they mess with nature. They muck up the planet.

But, boy, are they fun to build. The sheer joy of watching that water inch higher and higher: damming streams was one of my great pleasures as a child. But we always ended the play with tearing the dam down, returning things to normal.

In his classic work *Homo Ludens*, Dutch historian Johan Huizinga shows that the madness of modern life can be read as play that simply got out of hand. The rightful use of a steam turbine is, as the mathematician Hero demonstrated in first-century Alexandria, a child's toy, a lovely distraction. Harnessing that power is either a gamble (and from our modern perspective, brave and farsighted) or (from the Greek perspective) a colossal failure of judgement. Obviously, it would be absurd to condemn all progress, but progress of a certain technological kind, the kind that can quite easily lead to disaster, mayhem, dynamite, atomic bombs is pursued by people blinded, optimistic, greedy but still eager to play. The kind who ruin a Monopoly game through their sheer fanaticism, their unwillingness to see it's all . . . just a game. Though the English pride themselves on their sense of humour, they treat 'progress' as something beyond a joke. And yet we all believe there is some sort of link between good humour and good judgement (as we'll see later, this was how Ransome judged Lenin), but I think this misses out a link: the incongruous.* Good judgement requires an eye for the incongruous, and a lot of – but not all – humour revolves around seeing incongruities and calling them out.†

Whether you call out the madness or not is another fork in the path. Which is why we return to childhood. Which is why we look at our own childhood selves for guidance. Who hasn't said, 'I certainly didn't imagine I'd be doing this when I was a kid'? Which usually means being a lawyer or a tax inspector – careers that most children show a healthy aversion for. The use of childhood as a benchmark for honesty and clear-sightedness remains. That this is a romanticism doesn't seem to dent its appeal.

Childhood means a pristine state of self. What we apprehend in childhood is without the filters of societal pressure and coercion. Our real selves, we fondly think.

---

* This idea was stimulated by Idries Shah's *Knowing How to Know* and his writing on incongruity.
† But not *all* humour. Bullying, sarcastic and weakness-identifying humour needs only the emotional antennae of the sociopath.

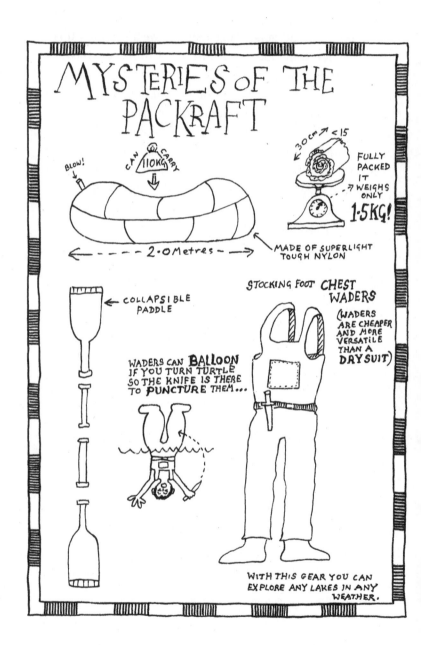

MYSTERIES of THE PACKRAFT

CAN CARRY 110KG

Blow!

30cm → < 15

FULLY PACKED IT WEIGHS ONLY **1·5KG!**

←- - - 2·0 Metres -→

MADE OF SUPERLIGHT TOUGH NYLON

← COLLAPSIBLE PADDLE

STOCKING FOOT **CHEST WADERS**

(WADERS ARE CHEAPER AND MORE VERSATILE THAN A **DRYSUIT**)

WADERS CAN **BALLOON** IF YOU TURN TURTLE SO THE KNIFE IS THERE TO **PUNCTURE** THEM...

WITH THIS GEAR YOU CAN EXPLORE ANY LAKES IN ANY WEATHER.

LOST ISLANDS

I arrived at Haweswater at midnight after a long wet drive from the south. I travelled the new road along its southern shore, constructed in the 1930s to replace the old road on the northern shore. I passed the dark and silent Haweswater Hotel, which has something remote and of *The Shining* about it, a replacement for the drowned Dun Bull Inn on the old north shore. A posh hotel replaces an ancient pub, still posh-ish. Again, the centralising effect of the dam, and of all centralising moves, is to overly concentrate power and wealth. Not much good comes of it.

And where to park? Which is the modern mantra of the Lakes, especially in these just post-Covid times with the place inundated with tourists in their camper wagons and bloated SUVs. I hove into an old quarry and slept till dawn.

I woke and brewed coffee on the gravelly quarry floor, next to a puddle. I was new to the crouching that is such a part of camping. I'd been locked up at home, sensible, fearful and wary, like everyone else. Sitting in chairs and looking out the window. Not much crouching. With my steaming coffee I looked over the well-built wall that surrounded Haweswater. All I could see was mist, and I could feel it too, tangible, damp, condensing on my scarf. All I could hear was the charging, distantly troubling roar of streams entering into the lake.

My aim, Haweswater's one island, is called Wood Howe. A 'howe' is a tumulus or barrow, though just as likely now to mean a hill. Perhaps in many centuries past it was a hill with a barrow or grave upon it. Wood Howe was the tallest hill in the surrounding area of Mardale village and as such couldn't be ignored. You couldn't tear it down like the church, or transplant it like the graves in the cemetery. You had to leave it there as a reminder that man can never make the world perfect and when he tries he always fails. The island makes the almost ugly, scoured, emptying reservoir look sweet again. And all water looks marvellous with morning mist upon it. But I'm getting ahead of myself because at that moment the morning mist was everywhere still and I couldn't see a thing.

My first island was not an ancient geological feature of the landscape. It was only eighty-five years old. It was less an island than an ex-hill. But it was a perfect introduction because islands are never permanent, they are always changing. They are the bellwether of our lands, our existence, in the same way that the sinking of the Marshall Islands in Micronesia signals a sea-level rise and perhaps the first disastrous effects of climate change.* Islands are outliers by virtue of their very nature and we can scry our future in them better than we can in our crowded continents and teeming cities. I was learning that islands are either becoming or disappearing. I could hardly wait.

I was so excited my hands were shaking as I loaded my rucksack with a lightweight packraft, paddles that broke

---

* Bellwether is an appropriate term for a sheep farming area. It refers to the bell hung round the neck of a castrated ram – a wether – who would lead a flock of sheep and indicate its presence to the shepherd. Whereas a ram, with all the independence a full set of balls implies, could not be trusted.

down into sections, wetsuit and lifejacket. A packraft looks like a child's beach toy, a bright yellow raft of tiny dimensions. But closer inspection reveals it is more like those escape rafts in which downed pilots are sometimes found (sometimes alive, sometimes as mere skeletons in a baggy flying suit and life preserver) with an enlarged bump at the back to balance the bottom-heavy weight of the paddler's bottom. I had never used mine despite owning it for about five years. It had been rolled up, unused, a gift to myself (they are pricey for what they are). After two years of it lying there, I blew it up and was surprised at how well made it was and how natty the inflation system was.

A large cloth bag is attached to the boat via a hole about an inch in diameter. There is therefore none of that annoying resistance a normal valve gives. The raft makers cunningly realised that you can pretty much fill a raft with low-pressure air and the structure of the raft will hold it in place. So this big bag, which you fill with air and then squeeze manually into the raft, works very quickly to inflate the packraft. As the air very gently leaks out of the hole left when the bag is removed (the pressure being so low), you then secure it with a tight-fitting cap. You can then top up the raft through a blow-up pipe, rather like blowing up a sleeping mat. Because the airbag has done all the heavy lifting, it only takes a few puffs to make the raft as tight as a drum and as light as a beach ball (it weighs about 1.5 kilos, but spread out over a 1.5 metre by 1 metre shape it feels almost weightless).

One of the things I have grown to love about the packraft is the fact that it's pretty childish. Just like a mountain bike is. There's nothing 'adult' about it, unlike a sleek motorboat or a chunky Range Rover. Of course, it's no guarantee that you'll remain childlike and playful when you use these things, but it's a start. As you get older you're faced with the stark choice of getting grumpier and less playful and less curious about the world and more fearful or . . . the opposite.

In any case, boats were needed for this mission, so boats will get their due. Yes, I came to love that packraft over time, but on this, its first outing, I was nervous.

The best place to launch was down below The Rigg, a high nose of land covered with hundred-year-old conifers. The track up ran around the north side of the lake. I pounded up it, fuelled by adrenaline. Would I be seen from the opposite bank? Would I be stopped?

I was glad to be using a map again, the trusty 2½ inch. There are four that pretty much cover the Lake District (though the S.E. map cuts off Blake Holme island, one of the models for Arthur Ransome's Wild Cat Island). Good navigators can usually get by with the old 1 inch map (or 1:50,000, as it is now) but I have always preferred the greater detail of the 2½ inch. I had borrowed the maps from my father and was glad to see one dated to 1974 – perhaps the first time we visited the Lakes. The newest was from 1980, over forty years out of date. I can safely say nothing significant had changed, including the campsites and carparks. Using out of date maps is much more fun than using Google or anything up to the minute. For a start, you have to use your discretion and decide to navigate using whatever features are likely to have remained unchanged. You need to be a bit careful with woodland (which can be chopped down or fully regrown in a span of fifty years) but rivers, old buildings, mountains – they stay the same.

Off the main trail and into the woodland of The Rigg. The high spruce had been thinned out and almost immediately I came across a fire circle made from stones lifted from an ancient dry stone wall running alongside the path. And a bit further on, another fire, or the remains of one. And the hated insult of a knotted and discarded dog-shit bag. I had thought Haweswater remote, likely to be overlooked by the summer hordes (and double that for the last two years of stay-at-home holidaying) but I was wrong. Well, here at least I was wrong. What about the island?

It was a steep and tricky climb over fallen logs as I descended to the rocky beach. Breaking out from under the trees I saw that as the lake dropped another island was revealed, a triangular shape of graded stones that joined the main Wood Howe. The gap to the new island was about forty feet across, maybe less.

I wound through collapsed and fallen remains of stone walls and the lower shapes of compounds, huts and maybe houses. Rusty and weed-strewn was a winch, standing useless on the mud. It was the kind of winch I had seen used on beaches to pull boats ashore. In former times Haweswater was known for its angling, and to boil sometimes with 'schelly', a salmonid fish that Wordsworth called a 'sort of freshwater herring'.* Nets were used to haul it ashore. There are also Arctic char – one of the rarer fish in Britain. When Wordsworth,

---

* *Coregonus stigmaticus*, which feeds on small crustaceans and hardly ever takes anything an angler offers by way of bait.

in his *Guide to the Lakes*, talks of men fishing with nets and seeing great shoals of chevin (chub) passing under a bridge you get the impression that there were a lot more fish and a lot more fishermen than today.

The mist was rising slowly. I could now see clearly the wooded island and the mass of newly revealed gravel attached to it. All I had to do was blow up my boat and go for it.

But never having used the boat, I wondered if it would work properly. And made fearful by the United Utilities signs in the carpark that suggested you'd freeze to death within minutes of falling in the water or going swimming, I began to reason my way out of actually making a visit. 'This is reconnaissance,' I told myself and felt bad about my lack of nerve.

But climbing back up The Rigg, I found myself in a little meadow full of tunnel spider webs. One web touched another and all were illuminated by mist droplets and early morning sun. It was like walking through a field of fine cloud, still with a silver lining.

In the end, I tried out the packraft for the first time on Ullswater. Again Wordsworth is good here: 'Haweswater is a lesser Ullswater, with the advantage that it remains undefiled by the intrusion of bad taste.' The bad taste in Ullswater is confined mainly to the overpopulated banks, the clusters of dwellings trying to wrest some living from the lake and the cars crammed into every lay-by. I found a good spot near Pooley Bridge to inflate the packraft and use it for the first time.

The idea is that you carry your rucksack over the bow, but my rucksack had an ergonomic back that was nicely sculpted to slide off the bow and into the water. I stuck it between my legs as I clambered in; there was hardly any space at all for my feet. I'm going to get cramp in this, I thought.

But while paddling about like a man in a plastic coracle, I found immense peace. The lake was dead flat and the sun was out. I soon left the wild swimmers behind, towing their little swim bladders. The paddleboarders were elsewhere. The sun shone down and I *took it easy*. No heaving on the paddles, no splashing to kingdom come. This will be great, I thought. This will be fun.

So back to Haweswater at dusk this time. All kitted up, a couple of weeks later, I cut down the log-strewn cliff, more carefully now because there was less light and because nightfall brings on care and greater concern. At the muddy maze of old dry stone walls I saw that the triangular gravel island had grown in size. In fact, the level of the lake was so low that a narrow spit of mud attached it to the mainland. And seeing as Wood Howe was already joined to the gravel triangle, the island was *no more.*

It was a disappointment. The lake being low was also not good; it was a reminder of the big world with its big problems. These days, Haweswater sucks water from Heltondale, Swindale and Naddle – and still it can't keep up with demand. But the disappointment of Wood Howe no longer being an island, at least for the next few days, meant that I was no longer trespassing on an island or camping illegally on an island, which had been my intention. For though half of me sought escape from the authorities and jeered at their attempts to control the lakes and islands, the other half was a craven rule follower whose fragile ego feared even a mild telling-off. Oh, but that would change.

I squelched through mud and noticed I was not the first. Smaller feet, maybe in trainers, preceded mine. A long ancient wall ran up the beach from out of the mud and into the trees of the island. I sheltered behind it, again imagining I was being watched from the road. The last cars of the day, leaving the small carpark at the lake head, drove by, lights on, occupants thinking about tea or a pint and certainly not about me. In the gathering gloom I climbed up through the tangled woods to the top of the hill in the island's middle. There was a strong feline smell, maybe wildcat I hoped. Moss covered all stonework, the collapsing central wall, the fallen trees. Birch trees, holly bushes and airy oaks, not very large. One very ancient mossy birch was carved with the letters 'FA', and then I assumed the carver had given up as it definitely looked like the start of something rather than an acronym for *fuck all*.

I set up camp at the highest point, albeit a bit too near to a small cliff with a twenty-foot drop. But it was the flattest spot. I could see right out of the tree cover to the road. There were no more cars. I was alone.

My first island! Well, not really an island, but still, a first of some sort. I spent a while searching for a good tent spot. When you haven't camped for some time there is a feeling that the tent won't stay up, that halfway through the night it'll collapse or blow away. You put in more pegs than you need, tighten lines. All that fear goes pretty quickly but I experienced it again that night. I slept badly and awoke at dawn. While I was brewing a cup of tea on my tiny gas stove I heard voices.

Like Robinson Crusoe, I grew fearful of the interlopers. I ducked down but they were coming up the slope. Almost

upon my tent now, a youngish bloke and an older one following. Both in fell running gear: clingy leggings and trainers
with grip. Were they blind? Or just being polite? I had to
speak, 'Er, hello, nice day for it.'

'Oh, aye,' said the older one. 'You camp here last night?'

I looked hard and saw only encouragement in his face.

'I did.'

'Looks great. Me and my son are out climbing Howes.
That's our name you see. Howe. And a howe, you know, is
a hill in the Lakes and this being Wood Howe we set out to
climb it when I saw the water was down.'

'How many have you done?'

'Forty-three.'

The son was looking at his mobile while we yakked, and
said, 'Never known it to be connected before.'

'How come your son always has a better phone than you?'
the man joked. 'Well, we'll be leaving you to it. Not bad,' he
said looking at his watch. 'Got one before 9 a.m.' And with
that they disappeared back down the slope and off the island.

The whole time I was talking to the Howes, father and son,
I didn't realise the woolly hat I was wearing had extended
high up on my head like a strange cone. They never said a
word.

COURAGE

Fathers travel with their sons and hope they can either teach
them something useful or pass something on, maybe the
ability to enjoy what the father enjoys. Ransome's father
managed to pass on a love of books and fishing to his son,

though Arthur was resistant to both in the beginning. In fact, it was only with his father's death that he began to take on his father's interests.

But though it's nice to do things with your son, this pales in significance compared to the real task of parenthood: instilling courage. All the other virtues – tolerance and generosity especially come to mind – require courage to be of any use. Generosity is actually intimately connected to courage; the miser is always scared of losing what he has, while the generous person opens his arms to the world. However, we adults are usually not at all clear on how to teach courage, if indeed it can be taught in the normal sense of the word. Maybe it is caught instead? By osmosis perhaps? Whatever the method, the main problem is often the starting point, when parents fail to realise their own journey from fear to courage was long and hard too. They try to get their kid to be brave instantly, and are ashamed (a bit) if their child turns out to be a natural born coward. Which actually should be the starting point: all kids are born cowards. Sorry, but it's true – either that or they are foolhardy (and die, get injured or quickly learn). People who survive start out timid, put out feelers, get some confidence and gradually expand their field of operation. And over time they minimise the situations in which they act in a cowardly way.

Ransome's biography is full of excuses for timid youthful behaviour when none are needed. And replete with instances of real courage, usually while he was a foreign correspondent. He clearly believed that courage is some sort of fixed quality, a gold standard of behaviour that you either have or you don't. In reality, it is an ever-fluctuating quality (affected as much by cold and lack of food as anything else), which, over time, we gradually manage to control and use. Only by knowing how much of an effect the environment has on our behaviour are we then able to learn how much of courage is simply an extension of what is considered 'normal' for a certain situation and how much is derived from some inner decision. Mostly, we underestimate the environmental factors in our behaviour. Which brings me back to the earlier discussion of 'the fork', the moment in life when you either give up and stop being open to the world and start to shut down, get grumpy, reduce learning experiences, do only what you have done before . . .

Because the fork is a test of courage. You've been courageous. You've got this far and things aren't quite what you hoped or expected they would be. And time is marching on. You aren't getting any younger. So you decide to stop moving on and start the digging in; what was provisional becomes absolute. People who were once given the benefit of the doubt, aren't anymore. Things that might have been treated with humour, because it wasn't worth losing your sense of humour over *anything*, now seem deadly serious. I remember reading Julian Barnes talking about Kingsley Amis who overnight, he felt, went from being a witty and clever man to being . . . a bore. He had taken the right fork, or maybe the left; whichever one it was, it led to false certainty – the hallowed playing fields of the bore, which is really the place where people who have lost their courage go to die.

For the decision to cease to be open, to cease to want to learn, to challenge yourself – all these are failures of courage, and a reversion to the timidity of the small boy clinging to the side of the swimming pool, unable to let go and risk getting his head wet. After such a decision one is never really happy with the adult world. It has failed you. The only people you can revere are those who reject the adult world: children, revolutionaries, outlaws, pirates . . .

And this is exactly the trajectory of Ransome. He leaves home and becomes a bohemian in London but marries the first woman who says yes to him (after protracted and fruitless sieges laid upon both Barbara and Dora Collingwood). However, she proves hard to handle so he runs away to Russia where he gets caught up in the First World War, which gives him a very good reason to stay away. Then he is swept up by the Russian Revolution. People find it odd that a man devoid of political interest, more or less a natural High Tory, should have been so enamoured of the Revolution that he married it: his second wife was the convinced revolutionary and Trotsky's secretary, Evgenia Shelepina.* All the revolutionaries liked this useful idiot who played chess with them and wrote what they told him about the revolutionary struggle. Lenin, no doubt, had given the OK and Ransome was never short of fulsome when writing about him. Like most children, Ransome had no understanding of real power (as opposed to the power of rhetoric) – of why it was attractive or how to deploy it. (Neither, of course, did Trotsky have a complete grasp of the subject, choosing to be away from Moscow on the day of Lenin's funeral, while Stalin, then almost unknown in the wider sphere, took care to hoist one corner of the coffin to his shoulder . . .)

Ransome then went on to write about Chinese warlords

---

* Evgenia was notoriously hard to please when it came to writing. She was fabulously dismissive of all of Ransome's work, only changing her tune after successful publication. But perhaps, compared to editing Trotsky, Ransome's work was a little underpowered . . .

and pirates (who he used to great effect in one of my favourite novels, *Missee Lee*) while covering the Chinese Civil War
for the *Guardian* before retiring to the Lake District to
write about a retired 'pirate' – Captain Flint, and, of course,
children.* In every spare moment he went fishing or sailing,
the childhood passions he loved so much.

His courage did not fail him. Rather, he misunderstood
that courage isn't a quality of character but a learnt attribute
that is used to live a better life as a better person. Quite
simply, it makes more sense to have courage; cowardice just
doesn't pay. Because Ransome overvalued courage he failed
to discern its reality and therefore was always at its mercy,
either driving himself to be foolhardy (as in his earlier days),
or the opposite, when, as an older man he retreated into a
second childhood of outdoor fun. But as a little boy who
never grew up he became somewhat crabbed and twisted
with age when the world refused to stay the same as his
idyllic childhood.

When the Altounyan children – the real-life models for
the Swallows and the Amazons – turned out different to
the fictional Walker children, he took against them. The
Altounyans are given recognition at the beginning of *Swallows and Amazons* in the dedication 'to the six for whom it
was written in return for a pair of slippers', as it was their
introduction to Arthur that helped give form to his first Lake
District novel. Though, as we'll discover, the books are more
about *his* childhood than theirs, these lively half-English,

---

* It is never entirely clear what Captain Flint did except that he is a man
of the world with more business flair than Ransome. He is certainly not a
journalist, a profession Ransome detested.

half-Armenian kids were an essential element in the whole Swallows and Amazons enterprise. Why he turned on them is the subject of much speculation. It could be the middle-aged resentment of a man whose own child has failed to come up to expectations, or it could be seen as a covert attack on their father who had a) failed to cure Ransome of his ulcer despite persuading him that he could, and b) married Dora Collingwood when she should really have married him. *

FOOTSTEPS

I explored the island. It was my first such exploration on this trip and I wanted to do it properly. Then I realised it was no different to the time I explored my first island, aged eight – Compass Island (as named by me), a piece of Warwickshire woodland that was surrounded by two streams and a connecting ditch. To get there entailed leaping a barbed wire fence sagging over the ditch water; miscalculate and this cruel, rusted steel would pull you down into the beige waters of the sluggish, overfull ditch. The boggy, flat island was ringed with willow trees. I walked about and made notes in my little notebook; now I did the same.

I knew that this island had once been a hill rising above Mardale, so it was an odd kind of an island – an ex-hill, an ex-bit-of-land – and as such it betrayed the lack of symmetry you might expect from something arbitrarily cut off and

---

* Dr Altounyan persuaded the gullible Ransome to book an expensive trip to Syria where he had his clinic. Not surprisingly, what with vaccinations, heat and foreign food, Ransome ended up worse off than when he left.

without centuries of smoothing at work on its protuberances. The single stone wall that ran like a saurian spine up its centre divided the place into an interesting lower series of rocky levels and the curving wooded dome of the opposite side. If you're familiar with the Lego Death Star model – it reminded me of that. There was little undergrowth – the wood of birch, hazel and sycamore was too mature for that.

It was about an acre, so maybe a couple of hundred metres, in length. I knew nothing about such places then, but it seemed a good size. In a way, it was all knowable just by standing in a single spot. By this, I mean you could pretty much see the water all around the island without walking from this high point. But there was a great amount of detail you risked missing if you assumed that seeing its fullest extent was equivalent to knowing the island. I didn't know then that the only way to know an island is to do a Crusoe; that is, walk its entire circumference and throw in a good number of cross-island zigzags for good measure too. However, if walking the circumference you run the risk of mistaking your own prints for those of an intruder. Indeed, this is the seminal moment in *Robinson Crusoe* itself (which is, let's face it, fairly workaday, designed as it was to persuade people it was a non-fiction memoir . . . like this one), when the double we all live with comes almost into existence in the solitary conditions of an uninhabited island.

Since most of us are divided selves, the metaphor of the identical twin or the double captures our unconscious interest. I would say that people are generally more intrigued by the idea of an identical twin than the notion deserves, likewise the double. Borges, in his famous taxonomy of the fantastic, the essay 'Los Cuatro Ciclos' ('The Four Cycles'), declared there were only four stories: time travel, the double, the work within the work and dream into reality. And often the double is a doorway into the other three. When we mistake our own reflection in an unsuspected mirror and believe for a moment we are seeing a stranger, or when we mistake our own footprint for that of an interloper, we give brief physical reality to an alternative history, past, present and future – an interstitial hole in reality through which we perceive the realer and more subtle knowledge that we are merely the stories we tell ourselves, or that others tell us, or are being told about us, and nothing more . . .

There were a few camp spots and a ring of stones signifying a fire – but last used a long while ago, with hardly any blackened sticks. My guess was that Wood Howe was pretty rarely visited as long as the waters were up. I found mysterious grids of wire – pillow-sized rectangular sections of fence material that looked like leftovers from a biological survey. Maybe the utilities company checking to see if wildcats lived on the island.

I walked back along the lake edge, finding a way worn into the side. It was like a path across a steep snow field: at first you think it'll be impossible to climb, it looks almost vertical, and then you see the way a gently rising path has been excised into the snow face, like those roads that wind through the Himalayas clinging impossibly to the rock face. (I realise that's a double metaphor but, what the hell, I'll take my chances.) The path seemed miraculous and was a joy to walk along. I've often found that paths in unlikely places, which make somewhere difficult and dangerous accessible, bring the greatest joy.

And walking along this path, I could not help but notice

a huge bird circling overhead. It was without doubt a golden eagle. Now my joy was overflowing, exciting, a little intense. The long, thick, squared-off wings with crude finger feathers at the end and the circling flap-free flight – not to mention its sheer size – all told me it was an eagle. I did not know at the time but England's last resident golden eagle had lived at Haweswater until its presumed death in 2016. But there had been reports of golden eagles moonlighting from Scotland. Perhaps this one was too. Seeing an eagle, preferably on a sunny day, seems like an omen of nothing but good.

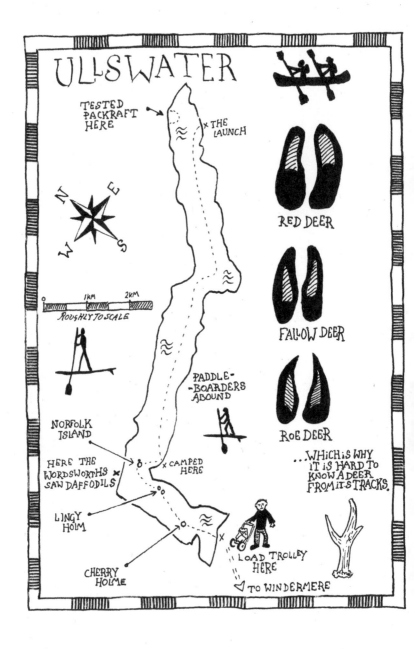

THREE

In Memory of Norman

Lake: Ullswater, 62.4 metres deep, 11.8 kilometres long,
8.94 square kilometres
Islands: Norfolk Island, Cherry Holm, Wall Holm,
Lingy Holm, Kalila, Dimna

I had tested the packraft in Ullswater but then I came back
with Mark and a much larger canoe. Mark was a forester
friend whom I had known since childhood. That carries
certain advantages and certain disadvantages when it comes
to travelling together. I wanted company, craved it almost at
this stage of the adventure. The episodic nature of exploring
islands broke any rhythm, any structure. And when you're
out on your own, you are hungry for any kind of structure.
And companionship is an automatic structure builder.

We left our cars at a campsite and loaded the inflatable
canoe onto its trolley. This was a sturdy portable luggage
trolley that I'd been given by a Japanese teacher in 1995. I'd
been advised by the writer Tahir Shah to get the biggest,
toughest and strongest luggage carrier I could find as they
are *not included in your weigh-in limit*. This was a bit before
every suitcase came with wheels. And actually the advice

is pretty good, as wheels really eat into the size and weight of a suitcase. But here, twenty-five years on, the trolley was going to come into its own. It had been resting in the garage in my parents' house all this time and I recovered it during a clear-out. Immediately, I realised I could use it to trolley the inflatable canoe between lakes.

Trolleys have always appealed to me. I once towed one across a part of the Sahara Desert. And I've noticed that people at festivals now use those American yard trolleys to move stuff about – very Burning Man, but also very sensible. If the ground has been levelled, or is already level, as in a desert, a trolley is a very efficient device. A trolley is also something that appeals to children, just like an inflatable boat does. And when the adult world lets us down, we retreat to those things that didn't.

I was always perplexed by that biblical injunction to 'put away childish things'; isn't that all we've got to hang on to? Our only beacon for an authentic life?

My octogenarian father took one look at the trolley and said, 'That'll shake to pieces in a couple of miles.' I remained an optimist. I *liked* the trolley, ergo it would survive and thrive under my care. But now, trundling from the field to the lakeside with the huge, rolled, black plastic bulk of the inflatable canoe attached by numerous bungee cords and straps with paddles and pump thrown in (this inflatable needed a large hand pump rather than the elegant bag system of the packraft), the trolley was both unstable and taking a beating from the uneven ground. Oddly enough, I looked forward to proving my father both right *and* wrong. Maybe a bit of each. I'm always trying to max out on available experience.

At the edge of the lake (which in Ullswater is close to roads on both sides) we unrolled the canoe, filled it with air and found out the right-hand bladder was punctured.

'When was the last time you used this?' asked Mark.

'About four years ago. It was punctured then too. But I mended it last week.'

Which I had, but something was wrong, maybe the valve. In the end, after hours of faffing, we decided to go with the slow leak and pump up every time we got a chance.

Ullswater has, officially, four islands. And it's a busy lake so the chances of those islands being pristine and empty were remote from the outset. Two steamers churn in a stately fashion up and down the nine-mile length of the lake. They are not noisy steamers, they're not like the odd powerboat that coursed by – loud, pointless and manned by a couple of dickheads, or one dickhead and his kids.* I've been in power-boats: they are exciting and fun for thirty seconds and then – bump, bump, bump as you hit the waves – they become boring. Working powerboats I can just about tolerate, but the roaring, wave-making tugboat of fun should be banned, I think, along with jet skis, which are just another invention of Satan. You see the owners just trolling back and forth; and it is no accident that *being a troll* is the major occupation of modern life for people who have lost the plot. Round them all up and incarcerate them all on St Kilda. Let them survive on scavenged stormy petrels and other nauseous seabirds. The time for jesting is over.

---

* An extract from my diary of that day reads: 'I hadn't been in the Lake District twenty-four hours before I realised it was a place that attracted WANKERS . . .'

And yet I am fascinated by record-breaking speedboats. Indeed, a whole strand of my interest in the Lake District stems from knowing it was the place where Henry Segrave, Edward Spurr (who worked with T.E. Lawrence) and Malcolm and Donald Campbell had tried to beat the world water speed record. The lakes chosen were Windermere, Coniston and Ullswater. I think it is the singularity of it, the ultimate statement of being an individual, that appeals to me. Is it any wonder that world land speed and water speed records have been utterly dominated by British and American contenders? No other country apart from Australia seems the slightest bit interested in how fast you can go on land and water, but it has consumed the lives, literally, of many Anglo-Saxons.

And yet when you look into the lives of the great record breakers, they are oddballs, real eccentrics who were often barred from the usual outlets for speed freaks. Malcolm Campbell was considered 'too clumsy' to be a fighter pilot. His son, Donald, was also barred from the RAF because of heart problems. Segrave called himself 'the world's worst pilot, always made a mess of landing'. In a sense, they're all Eddie the Eagles but with added horsepower.

As a child (ah, that again), at the very same time as I was beginning to love Arthur Ransome I bought a hardback book called *The Record Breakers* for only 17½p in the discount section of WHSmith in Stratford. There was a TV show of that name that revolved around a book I desperately yearned to own – the annual *Guinness Book of Records*. But this popular item was a) vastly expensive, and, b) disdained by my father and mother. With trembling eagerness, I bought the book without even investigating its contents.

With a kind of magical thinking, I willed the book to

be a version of the Guinness compilation of world records. In fact, it was much more interesting and influential. I still have the same copy on my bookshelf next to me as I write. *The Record Breakers* is a first-person account by Leo Villa, the head mechanic for both Malcolm and Donald Campbell. It covered most of the twentieth century and was the prism through which I later viewed major events such as both world wars, the Great Depression, the threat of communism and the swinging Sixties. I first encountered them all through the distorting lens of trying to go as fast as possible on land and water. Indeed, for me, these great world-shattering events were mere interludes in the pursuit of speed.

At the same time as Arthur Ransome was writing about Swallows and Amazons and sailing his own and other people's boats on Windermere and Coniston, Segrave and Campbell were tearing up and down these lakes at a hundred miles an hour. Just at the moment that nostalgia for sail over steam ('steam gives way to sail, that's the rule' is one of the mantras of Captain John, who is an idealised stand-in for the youthful Ransome) is beginning, quite possibly aided by the appearance of monstrously fast speedboats, we see a series of children's books that, like those of Enid Blyton, are completely removed from 1930s 'reality'. In a sense, they hark back to the Edwardian days before the First World War and Ransome's own childhood, when faith in the enlightenment project was still intact.

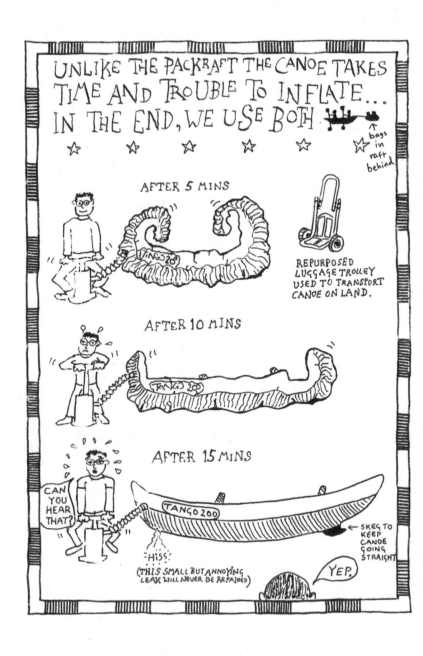

And the speedboaters were the opposite of all that sailing and exploring (though Malcolm Campbell did go exploring for buried treasure on several occasions during his eventful life); they were all grubby and dirty and eagerly courted death. Just as children catch on very early to sexual attractiveness, they also intuit the whiff of death and the contradictory messages of self-destruction and self-transcendence that death metaphorically signals. It seems entirely appropriate that T.E. Lawrence was working with Edward Spurr on a superfast boat shortly before his own death.

You sense the spirit of Icarus: at the moment before Campbell's boat crashes, it tries to take off, to fly. Indeed, 'tramping' – shuddering from sponson to sponson as the speedboat accelerates – is usually a prelude to a doomed attempt at flight. But it's the last thing the pilot wants. Being constrained and bound to earth, yet fuelling oneself and one's machine with the ingredients of flight, means that some kind of terrible conflict of energies is involved, something wholly unnatural. And, especially in the case of waterborne attempts, it very often leads to death. Since half of literature is peering into the abyss of death, perhaps that explains at least some of the fascination I have.

Or is it childhood again?

I like to imagine that Ransome was present, turning his back from the water, lighting his pipe, ignoring the furious noise and the bow wave from Segrave's boat as it smashes the water speed record in 1930 on Windermere. And what were his thoughts on that speed king's death only minutes later?

Here, on Ullswater, the first record was set by Donald
Campbell in 1955 when he became the first person to smash
the 200mph barrier on water. The MP Wavell Wakefield, a
canny businessman who was chairman of an engineering
firm as well as the Ullswater steamer company, had lured
Campbell to Ullswater with the offer of help in building
Campbell's new speedboat, the jet engine Bluebird K7. The
two steamers Mark and I had seen going about their stately
and unconcerned business earlier were the same ones that
had been operating so many years earlier, when Campbell
broke the record.[*]

Though Donald's father, Malcolm, had always preferred
Coniston, Donald favoured Ullswater for its greater length
and absence of the large islands Windermere had. He was
not bothered by the dogleg in the middle that meant making
a slight turn. Leo Villa sat next to him on the test runs and
described the experience as 'exciting but bloody frightening'.
After numerous changes and further tests, Campbell sped up
Ullswater, clocking 202mph, a new world record.[†]

Gear piled up on the beach always looks *way too much* for
the canoe. But somehow it all fits in. However, this time we
were pretty cramped. Mark suggested using the packraft as
a kind of bumboat attached by cord to the back of the canoe
and carrying all our gear. That way, we could spread out in
the canoe and be able to avoid being trapped by rucksacks
and boots. The addition of a bright yellow 'tender' popping

---

[*] Indeed one of them, *Lady of the Lake*, built in 1877, is arguably the oldest
passenger steamer still in regular use anywhere in the world.

[†] There is now a speed limit on Ullswater of 10mph. Still fast enough to
cause quite a bow wave.

along behind us meant by the time we were underway we were already quite a sight, a presence on the largely uneccentric present-day waters of Ullswater.

Most boatmen are hugely conventional. It's not as if there are laws against travelling in weird and whacky contraptions, but people like to fit in. Especially where they feel a little nervous, like people do on water, a place where they might drown. Take the new interest in paddleboarding, which is a benevolent form of speedboating in the sense that it is as meaningless as casual motorboating. Person A sees paddleboard X in advert, or spots Person B using paddleboard Y, and then buys all the kit and perhaps goes out with mates C, D and E. (I witnessed youngish people, the kind with new reg cars and decent bods and haircuts, gathering after work to go paddleboarding en masse on Ullswater. It builds core strength and is less boring than wild swimming, I guess.) But they all have similar gear. Trendy wild swimmers are the same too – with a special little swim bladder to tow behind them with their mobile phone and dry kecks inside, or maybe just a tiny bottle of champagne to celebrate landing on an island.

You have thoughts like this when the sun is reflecting off the water in ten thousand wonderful shards of white light, not harsh enough to cause eyestrain but enough to make one feel Caribbean, languid, drifting, at home yet utterly released.

And so, mid-lake, Mark and I drifted. A touch of the paddle, here, a touch of the paddle, there. Mark was into taking it easy, too. He had spent a sizable chunk of his formative working years alone in a large wood, strimming, sawing, felling, planning, eradicating grey squirrels, and eating his packed lunch off the bonnet of a yellow tractor.

All that alone time had turned him into a philosopher, which was one of the reasons (apart from his useful knowledge of trees – there're lots of trees on islands) I had asked him along. I could tell Mark was happy taking it real easy. There was no subconscious rushing of the kind you get from people with regular nine to five jobs who get out into the wilderness for their therapeutic escape time. Although Mark's job was actually nine to five now, running the forestry department of a big national organisation, he was deeply imbued with the spirit of the tree-dwelling recluse, the hermit, the old boy with a straw dangling from his mouth who watches the world go by.

People who spend a lot of time observing others have never wasted their lives, yet the culture enjoins us to engage continuously . . . and to judge, yes, to judge the people of the present, the past and even the future. But here Mark and I were, simply watching, drifting and watching.

'Pretty good this,' said Mark.

'Yep.'

'Did I ever tell you about the time an oyster bit my finger?'

'No, tell on.'

Yes, all the time in the world for catching up on things the modern world tries to bulldoze aside in favour of Netflix and Disney+. It was one among several reasons why I enjoyed Mark's company, his seemingly endless stream of unique experiences.

'Did I mention about the time I asked for some fork handles?'

Mark explained the *Two Ronnies* sketch, which I vaguely remembered, where a man goes into a hardware shop and asks for fork handles and the man thinks he wants four candles. Anyway, one day, not long ago, Mark found himself with a fork that needed a new handle. So he went into a shop that sold cutlery and other such goods and asked for 'fork handles'. The man behind the counter changed colour and ranted, 'Oh, you think I haven't heard that one before? Think you're original, do you? Well, I can tell you . . .' and he did. When he had finished Mark told him, 'I've waited twenty years to be able to say this, and I really do want a fork handle' – and he held up the damaged fork. 'He calmed down after that and was quite friendly by the end,' Mark said.

I decided then and there that paddling a canoe as slowly as possible, just enough to stay on course, was my absolute favourite activity. It was even better than sailing on a river when there is almost no breeze (which oddly enough I had also done with Mark many years earlier, and the memory had remained as the apogee of boating without the windy racket and ear-splitting flappery of most sailing). I decided that I would devote a good part of my leisure time to seeking out places where I could minimally propel myself along in a canoe. You see, all these years I'd been trying to go as fast as possible. Giving myself RSI on one elbow among other things. It was all so simple. Point yourself in the right direction and go as slowly as you can . . . the sun and warmth and gentle waves . . . going down that lake was pure pleasure . . .

The wind must absolutely not be too high. Here, there were only the faintest of cat's-paws, as if a thousand silver teaspoons were laid out in a carpet for an instant, caught by the sun's largesse; then that quadrant of breeze passed and all was flat again. The boat, slowly deflating, made no noise in its transit owing to its soft cloth exterior. One of the bugbears of an aluminium canoe is the pinging it makes as it slices through water (though some claim to be intoxicated by the noise, a joyous spring-like gurgling at the bow, a recording of the water of life, a signal that adventure is nigh, they say). But I prefer to sneak through the flat calm with scarce a murmur. Or even a splash of paddle. Mark was good at this, he propelled a dry ship and I only seemed to land drips on him rather than noisily back into the lake.

NORFOLK ISLAND?

Norfolk Island was the first stop. But it was way down the other end of the lake. We had to keep paddling albeit very slowly and steadily. Happily, the miracle of slow and steady is that you just can't help getting there in the end . . . We stopped en route when we rounded Skelly Neb (a nose of land where no doubt the elusive skelly had once been landed) and zigzagged across to take a closer look at a plaque cemented onto the rock wall of Kailpot Crag. It commemorated Lord Birkett, who, in the 1960s, led a spirited and successful defeat of the evil Manchester Corporation, which had tried to get a bill through parliament to turn Ullswater into a reservoir (like the bill in the 1920s that had drowned Mardale).

> In Memory of
> Norman William Birkett
> Baron of Ulverston
> He loved Ullswater
> He strove to
> maintain its beauty
> for all to enjoy

Thank the gods for Norman, I say, thank them fivefold. I'd already seen the slight death pall that hung over Haweswater, the neglectful way it was allowed to 'draw down' and puddle in the initial greedily increased extent of itself. Ullswater remains one of the most beautiful of the lakes with its balance of woodland, craggy overhangs, small beaches and surrounding hills. Imagine it chain-linked and sucked dry, so some manky bastard can have more than one shower a week – no thanks!

Initially, because I am something of an anarchist with an anarchist's dislike of the nobility, I was disdainful of Norman being a baron. But on reflection, I realised that the more hereditary peers we had, the better the chance we had of saving places such as Ullswater from well-meaning destruction. Since hereditary peers were an endangered species themselves, they would, quite naturally, side with all other things in danger of extinction.

I was destined, in a week or so, to attend Camp Good Life – a kind of eco/organic/hipster festival run by a Welsh baronet from his ancestral castle in Hawarden. I looked forward to seeing how the aristocracy were dealing with the current malaise. I would be going there with my paddling head on, which I rather relished as it would give me something to talk about – which you need when people ask you at a festival what you're doing. Which they do.

Norfolk Island, named after the Duke of Norfolk, is just across from Glencoyne Bay, where William and Dorothy Wordsworth saw the famous daffodils that both wrote about. I have to admit to a prejudice against that poem, partly because it had been lampooned everywhere when I was growing up (even in the *Beano* comic) and also because

William was with his sister when he saw the daffodils and so he hadn't 'wandered lonely as a cloud.'* I love Wordsworth as a concept, though; he's a true Beat Poet whose openness is also his fatal weak spot. In any case, the first serious island beckoned after the joined-up experience of Wood Howe. But as it came into view we could see the bright colours of waterproofs and a column of smoke: people were already in possession of the place. Ah, the moment of decision.

'What about over there?' Mark pointed to a beach and a small bay on the south side of the lake. 'Maybe we could wait until they've gone?'

'If they go.'

We landed on the beach and owing to our general unfamiliarity with landing on rocky, slippery places (and this being the first landing we had made in our current two-boat format), Mark slipped and fell hard on the rocks as we were getting out. He fell with the extra heaviness you have when you get older. As you age your centre of gravity seems to rise and falls become more serious.

'Are you OK?' I said anxiously.

'Yeah, I'm fine,' said Mark after a pause, his voice lower and more bass than usual. He walked up the beach rubbing his leg; he was never one to complain.

I took it as a sign to be extra careful. On the beach we set up camp and proceeded to make these rookie errors:

---

* A small and perhaps trivial objection but key to the weakness of the image – no cloud is lonely, as a single cloud glories in its dominance of the blue sky . . .

a. Not putting up the tent until dark and then finding out that . . .

b. my head torch batteries were flat owing to the head torch switching itself on in my bag. Despite my knowing it did this, I had not remembered to take out the batteries before packing it.

c. So, with no tent, I slept out in my bag and admittedly the stars were dense and brilliant to look at. I watched the Great Bear turning around the Pole Star until I fell asleep . . .

d. only to wake up at 3 a.m. when it was raining and then flailing around in an attempt to finally put up said tent (inside out) without a torch – until Mark called from his tent and offered his, bless him.

Before Mark offered me his torch I fumbled around in the dark, catching my foot on a rock I hadn't seen. 'Be careful,' I told myself, not just because of witnessing Mark's earlier fall, but because of the ominous tragicomic accident that befell Arthur Ransome's father.

Coming back from fishing near the village of Nibthwaite in the dark, he jammed and twisted his ankle between a rock and a discarded millstone, but optimistically assumed he had only sprained it. Fearing that it would 'seize up' and spoil his holiday, he manfully walked home on it and carried on as if it were fine, strapping up the swollen and bruised ankle each day. But he had actually broken a bone in his foot, which soon became infected with tuberculosis. In the end, he had to have his foot amputated, yet carried on as before. However, the infection spread, so then his leg below the knee had to be removed, and finally above the knee . . . Yet he refused to let it get him down. He had a cork prosthetic leg and a special tricycle adapted so he could trundle after his fellow grouse hunters and shoot while sitting in it. But the infection kept coming and he died a little while later. Arthur was thirteen, young for his age and still to discover our fathers don't know everything after all.

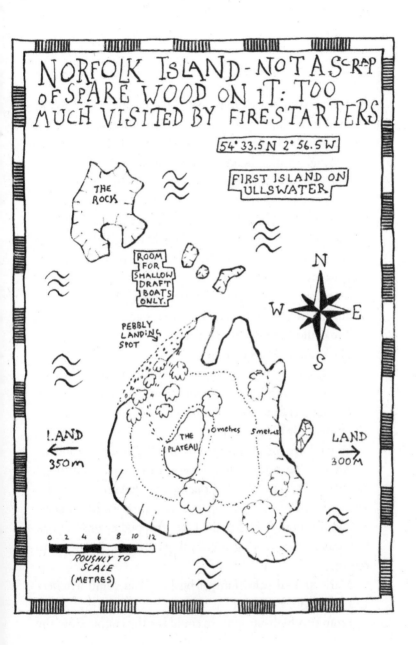

Getting to sleep wasn't that easy as the people on the island seemed to be having a rave. Not to mention a couple on the beach who had an enormous fire and their own music box going. Shouts, laughs, thumping music – the noises travelled far and fast across the still water. This was the tail end of summer. Maybe all these revellers were having a final bash before returning to university. At one point, the beach people got into their small powerboat and pushed off. I have to say, though, by the time the rain came there was silence everywhere . . .

Morning. The best time if it isn't raining, but it was.

'Just as well we didn't camp on the island,' said Mark.

'We could have joined the party.'

Mark ignored this comment.

'I'm surprised there are any trees left on that island,' I said.

'Well, technically you can chop any tree down thinner than seven centimetres in diameter.'

'Wow. Didn't know that.'

'*If* you have the permission of the landowner,' he added.

After taking our time to get ready, we climbed up through bracken to the top of Silver Crag for a better view of the lake. The early mist had long departed and now we had a good view down both halves of the lake. Propped against an oak tree was a Leki walking stick, still waiting for its owner to return.

Mark spotted some juniper bushes. 'You could live here and make gin,' he said.

From this high-up spot we could see the couple from the

beach, who were now asleep in their open boat as it drifted on the lake. They looked like children bewitched in a fairy story.

On the beach we found a pair of white tennis shoes, laces undone, waiting at the lapping shore. Maybe in their haste to get into the boat to sleep, the couple had left them behind. Would they return?

Such questions were just putting off our real purpose. More air into the slowly deflating side of the boat. And only a short rainy paddle to Norfolk Island, now deserted. The approach to a new island is always exciting, however small it is. If you suspect or know that there are people already on the island then the anticipation is dulled, the excitement void. The pure essence of island is uninhabited, pristine, waiting to be explored.

I savoured that excitement as we approached. I sensed that Mark was feeling the same thing as we were both silent and not making the usual quips that we both indulgently allow ourselves. That feeling of anticipation is in itself like a shot of pure childhood. Kids get excited about the unknown. Adults get excited about the known, about those familiar pleasures they are about to indulge in yet again; food, wine and sex come to mind. Adulthood is about pleasure, childhood is about exploration. I was thinking broadly here, in between quick paddle strokes.

We found a way through the rocks guarding the landing place. The island was small, maybe fifty metres long. The way up from the beach through the trees led to the top, where the grass was worn down to within an inch of its life. Ducks, probably, plus a fair few humans had done it. In its bare aspect, it was easy to see no one was on the island, but it felt like people might arrive any time. I wanted my perfect island to be more secure than this one. I rigged up a tarpaulin from the knotty oak and ancient willow trees on the beach and got a brew going.

A small kitchen tarp is the best extra bit of gear you can bring with you on a camping trip. Fixing food, opening rucksacks, changing socks, if done in the rain, are sorrowful exploits that lead to one place only: the total and utter inundation of your kit. Under the tarp you can live dry and breathe easy. One made of Cuben Fiber (or Dyneema, as it is also known) can weigh as little as 100 grams.

On one side, the island rose up several metres from the water in a long, steep slab of rock, with holly, ash, beech, oak and willow growing from whatever earth could accumulate there. The trees were somewhat hacked and reduced; we could see the still smoking fire circle the partygoers had created – and to their credit they had left no rubbish behind. When the children first arrive on Wild Cat Island in *Swallows and Amazons*, they're disappointed by a similar fire ring and stacked wood:

> Someone had had a fire here, and someone was meaning to have a fire again.
>   'Natives,' said Titty.*

After our exploration, a group of kayakers arrived with their cheery teacher/leader.

'Got a brew on for us then have you?' he said jauntily.

---

* Yes, a full discussion of this name and its change for the 2016 *Swallows and Amazons* movie will occur – but not just yet.

'No,' I replied, ever the bad sport. Hoping they'd leave.

Then two paddleboarders arrived and I was less grumpy. (People doing their own thing are fine but there's something about outdoor adventure guides and their guileless 'clients' I can't stand – and I've been both.)

'Natives'. In one word the Swallows dismiss the other users of the Lakes. Their fantasy is *so strong* that the Lake District of trippers and world record powerboats simply vanishes like the nearby shore in the mist. It is Ransome channelling his own childhood and superimposing it on the lives of the young Altounyan children. It is a childhood rendered into a superficially realistic fairy tale.

And yet it is also something the Lake District encourages. The natives are in such abundance in Rio (Ransome's name for Bowness) and other Lake District towns. The natives are in such abundance, yet the scenery is so beguiling – the mountains at the end of Ullswater, row in front of row diminishing with perfect proportion, enough to set the mind wandering and wondering, along with the lakes, and islands – that you very quickly slip into an alternative reality in which people who don't fit, the natives, are somehow reduced and the fog just lifting off the lake at dawn becomes much more important.

It is part of the considerable but invisible skill of Ransome that he devotes so much time to activities that may seem outwardly to be rather mundane: the sailing to the island, finding a landing place, the discovery of the Secret Harbour, fishing for perch, or swimming round the island. But he is giving these experiences their precise childhood value, which is very, very high. Yet he hasn't bloated them with a thriller element in the way that Blyton does; he's kept well within the realist tradition. And he isn't a charmer like Tolkien; there is something blunt in his description of places, something flat in his prose – perhaps the result of all that journalism, all that writing about the Russian Revolution, getting it straight and accurate.

It is the symbolic and perhaps also the magical significance of the island that gives power to these mundane acts, that sustains his descriptions and keeps us interested. That's why I could never really see the point of the second book in the series, *Swallowdale*; in it, the children camp on the mainland, not on the island. The mundane activities remain mundane. Indeed, only the exotic event of Roger getting to stay the night with the archaic charcoal burners really piqued my interest. Though I would never dare to agree that a Ransome book could be boring, *Swallowdale* edges in that direction. Without the island, or some other symbolic element, the intense pleasures of childhood cannot be communicated.

And now we were about to live again the intense pleasure of approaching another uninhabited island . . .

Our second stop, Lingy Holm, was an island in two parts. You could step, with care, across a tiny dividing gap of water that was too narrow for even a canoe. Heather, a rowan tree and a few scrub willows grew there. It was not an island with much cover but you could camp on it, just. People had. Mooching about, we carried on the conversation about the discarded tennis shoes we'd found earlier.

'Were you thinking of taking them?' asked Mark.

'No way. Well, maybe. They looked OK.'

'I once met my dad and he was proud to be wearing a

sheepskin hat he'd fished out of the Thames and some trainers he'd found floating in Cardiff Docks.'

'I'd have been proud too. Some of my most treasured kit
has been stuff I've found. Or been given as a cast-off.'

Found stuff, like the mountain of useful equipment
Crusoe takes from his wrecked ship, is always better than
bought stuff. The act of finding, and of finding a use for
what you've found, brings a living quality to the acquisition,
unlike the dead hand of money. It's a subtle thing and in no
way disparages the usefulness of bought things; nevertheless,
true magic can only inhere in the found or the given. One of
my grandfathers, a farmer, had a toolkit made up mainly of
odd tools he had acquired along the way, very few of them
bought. His penknife was one he'd found while walking his
land, perhaps left behind by people camping.

Wall Holm ('holm' is from the Old Norse *holmr*, meaning
small island) was bigger: 'Great for a glamp site,' said Mark.
'Enough room for six tents here.' We splashed ashore. There
was a lot of duck shit under foot, Wall Holm obviously being
a preferred roosting spot. There was also a nice inlet, rowans
and rushes, as well as two Corsican pines.

I was concerned that after only visiting three islands, we
were already becoming guidebook pedants, ticking boxes.
It was not meant to be like this, and later, on other lakes, it
wasn't. But that day, the weather was beautiful and warm (the
rain had stopped) and flotillas of similarly hued paddleboards
came up too close and too often for us to feel the necessary
aloneness you need for appreciating uninhabited islands.

A heart shape fashioned from shells hung from the taller
of the two pines.

This object, hung by some romantic soul, reminded me

of an aluminium plaque affixed to a magnolia tree on the top of Jarn Mound, just outside Oxford – a place where I loved to play when I was growing up. The plaque read 'I will always love you'. Plaque and tree are now long gone, but Sir Arthur Evans, the archaeologist who uncovered Knossos on Crete, knew how to make his mark. Jarn Mound was a wholly artificial hill, designed to offer outstanding views of Oxford. He employed twenty workmen in the 1930s to pile up a fifty-foot hill of earth. It took nearly three years to complete. Evans, who some accuse of a surfeit of creativity in rebuilding Knossos, obviously had caught something from the ancients – if only the knowledge that, better than words, building a real live hill ensures you leave something permanent behind. Hills, unlike buildings, require no maintenance and they can't easily be knocked down (presumably you'd need just as many workers to take it away as build it). And creating one gives some insight into the work needed to create ancient monuments.

In the gardens around the mound there was an artificial stone barrow we called The Bear Caves and a modern menhir that was good for climbing. The gardens were planted with rhododendrons and lots of exotic species and were a great place to play. Evans may have died childless but he provided a wonderful playground for the children of others.

Strangely enough, there was a persistent rumour that the earth for Jarn Mound came from the ornamental lake in the gardens of Evans's nearby house, a lake where I had once rowed about with Mark the gamekeeper's son and landed on an island – small and of bare earth, but the first island that, for me, bore some resemblance to those in Arthur Ransome's books.

FREUDIAN TRIP

Childhood. It's time to dig deeper. Who deeper than Freud? While his reputation divides people, his work remains compelling, to me at least. And there is a Lake District connection, of sorts: his daughter Anna was involved in teaching art therapy to the 'Windermere Children' – 300 Jews from Theresienstadt concentration camp who were settled for a while after the war at Windermere. Whether you think him a fraud or a genius, his popularising of the unconscious is vastly influential. And the use of the Oedipus myth to dramatise the essential problem of transition from fathers to sons has more than a little bearing on Ransome.

I wasn't surprised to discover that the first English use of the word 'unconscious' in the modern sense was made not far from Ullswater by Coleridge in his *Biographia Literaria* (which was in turn inspired by the philosophy of Schelling). The unconscious gradually becomes conscious as we learn more about ourselves. Personally, I use the word in the widest possible sense rather than the strict Freudian meaning. For me, the unconscious is all that is hidden from our knowledge of ourselves and our behaviour. It is thought to be revealed in dreams and in childhood trauma, but also in daydreams, cyclical behaviour, common mistakes, avoidance strategies, any desire to escape . . .

We typically interrogate our childhoods to gain information about our unconscious ambitions and inhibitions. For those who had a happy childhood, like me, it's a very pleasant process – a nostalgia fest with a bit of potential enlightenment thrown in. Those for whom looking back is too painful can't indulge in this 'method' as often.

For some reason, the ambitions we conceived in childhood have far more depth and power than those we think up later. The roots are not merely intellectual; they seem organic. I know that when I set out to write a book the subject must involve an image burnt deep into my mind. The subject must have an almost tangible quality. It can't be 'thin'. Usually, I have to have been turning the concept round and round for years, sometimes fifteen or more, before I get around to writing about it. And very often the roots of the idea can be found in some childhood obsession.

We connect childhood interests with those revealed in dreams: perhaps they offer pointers to our destiny. The ancient notion that we might have a destiny is reformatted in the endless scrying over childhood evidence of a calling or inclination we ought to pursue now we are grown up. The idea of 'fulfilling our potential' is really a modern version of following your destiny . . . maybe I really *was* supposed to be an ice artist/bonsai maker/local councillor . . .

That's why, I'm sure, modern generations hold off deciding as long as possible who 'we really are'. We need always to have an escape option available, an island we can swim to.

No doubt without Freud we wouldn't look so inquiringly at our childhood. It is to him we owe the idea of personality being acquired in childhood through the transition of five psychosexual stages. I won't list them as they sound funny written down as, indeed, even the word 'psychosexual' does. Is Freud suspect simply because he's given us so much to poke fun at? There's serious stuff in Freud, I have to repeat that.

But do we get our view of 'reality' in childhood? Isn't it that we discover, over time, just how far our initial fantasies hold true? In other words, we start from a fantastical fairy tale position and gradually watch as life bites chunks out of this. But then that isn't quite right, because deprived children, those whom we assume to have no illusions, actually have the worst set of illusions: that love is a word without meaning, that the world is a dangerous, horrible place, that no one can be trusted. The pessimist who lives in a highly developed modern state can afford to have such illusions, but those who rely on others must accept the world is a much kinder and empathetic planet. People who might doubt this should interrogate anyone who has biked or driven round the world – their tales of kindnesses received always vastly outnumber acts of hostility.*

Extreme atomism as a methodology, which of course has led to so many amazing discoveries, is by a sleight of mind taken to be a 'realer' version of everything. According to it, man alone – an island – is thought to be more real than the network of relationships that encompass us all.

---

* A man who had driven his family around the world in a van told me he had the kindest reception in Pakistan, the one country about which he had been so doubtful that he had driven through it alone, his wife and children waiting for him in India. 'My mistake,' he said. 'Ninety-eight per cent of the world are friendly and want to help.'

THE TROLLEY

Ullswater is picking up wind, and the sky is clouding over. The leaking air bladder seems to have reached a kind of state of equilibrium and has remained at the same fairly deflated level for a while now. The islet of Cherry Holm – circled, landed on (it is a large rock really) and left – and Kalila and Dimna, two islets that are now joined to the land, were the last of Ullswater's islands. We now had to get to Windermere, which was about eighteen miles away . . . using the trolley.

I was looking forward to the challenge of shifting our considerable tonnage of gear overland to the next lake. In our way was about five miles of walking to get to a possible first stop, Patterdale, before surmounting the foggy and fearsome 1,500-foot-high Kirkstone Pass. It was this pass that Arthur Ransome doggedly traversed when he ran away from his prep school, the Old College at Windermere. Tormented by a sports teacher for his inability to catch, he was pelted with cricket balls, which he vainly lunged after much to the hilarity of both his classmates and the vindictive teacher (but aren't all sports teachers sadists?). Small wonder he legged it.

In Ransome's autobiography considerable space is given over to explaining how it was undiagnosed short sight that led to him being a poor junior sportsman and in particular a boxer who could not defend himself. This is patently untrue if given even half a moment of thought. Plenty of boxers are short-sighted; it is after all only the close range that is important and a blur is a blur when a fist is moving fast.

The clue is that Ransome admitted he looked forward to a bloody nose so that the boxing session would then end; in other words, he didn't defend himself not because he couldn't see, but because a) he wasn't able to, and, b) defence would just lead to a longer session of being beaten up. Anyone who has practised boxing knows that the pain is bearable just as long as you are administering greater pain to your adversary. When it is the reverse it is intolerable. And when you are young you are naturally a coward; you only grow into courage as you mature.

We know that Ransome's father berated and insulted Arthur enough for the boy to be first scared and then scarred. There is no doubt the humble-bragging tone of the autobiography when it comes to acts of valour (or folly) is down to the childhood trauma of being called a 'coward'.

In a fit of sobbing and blind shame, Arthur fled the school and headed up Kirkstone Pass. But as the day waned he eventually calmed down and got the bus back to school. Perhaps it is an indication of their own guilt about a boy running away that the event caused neither punishment nor even a mention to his parents. It was simply allowed to be forgotten.

'I think we should get the bus,' said Mark, 'if there is one.'

'Well, maybe, but let's see if this trolley thing works first.'

At the end of the lake we deflated and rolled up the canoe into a very tight bundle. I loaded it high and narrow onto the trolley so it didn't wobble as much as before. Mark carried a yellow bag containing the paddles and pump. The first challenge was to traverse a damp hilly field of cows. Given that we were both full of beans at this early stage of the challenge, it was quite easy. We then embarked on a long gravel road that ran towards Patterdale, one of the many places in the Lakes that could be part of Tolkien's Shire.

My pack is heavy and I am pulling the trolley, switching from side to side. As it was my idea, I am happy to pull the trolley. Mark offers to do a stint but I decline. He knows not to ask again. I have locked myself into some kind of test. A mile, two miles and it's getting tougher, but when we leave the gravel and travel parallel to the main road on an undulating, muddy path strewn with stones and rooty trip-wires it becomes . . . much harder. I have to call for Mark's help at every incline, every patch of bad stones. It becomes quickly exhausting and the sense of the whole enterprise rapidly begins to drain. In a way I am perversely happy: all my trips involve these kind of moments and I have a sort of masochistic nostalgia for them. But at the same time I'm getting tired out, worn out even. When the going becomes this kind of heroic yet pathetic struggle (cars whizz by on the road below, emphasising our brutally slow progress) you start to make exit plans fast. Your mind strips out the fancy trimmings of the trip and cuts to the core. And add to that the fact that night will fall soon and we'll need to camp. I'm sweating and my body is both tormented by the pain of new exertions yet somehow eager to continue the punishment, but for how long? Mark stoically matches my pace. In his own quiet way he's a macho man and won't back down until I do.

More root-strewn paths, more rocks and rocky steps to go up and down. The sight of a brook running alongside the path alleviates our grim mood. The sight of water is always pleasing – a river means escape. Then onwards to a blob I've seen on the map: another lake sadly with no islands, which serves as a reservoir for Patterdale. And Patterdale it is, with the rain now falling. The edge of the lake is found and fallen upon after a heroic final struggle up a slight incline. It's amazing how a wheeled vehicle makes an average hill into a monster of gradient; even 4x4s struggle up hills a walker can stroll up easily. Room for thought on that one: 'the impact of wheels on the disappearance of personal resilience and initiative'. Perhaps the wheel-less empires were really the stronger, on an individual level, and perhaps wheels are the origin of tyranny?

I'm so tired I lie listless under the tarp – which I blunder-ingly put up, whipping my face with an errant bungee cord on two occasions, connecting to odd rocks and dusty tree boughs. It was narrow beach and we were almost camped on the path but I didn't care. I lay slumped and then made a Pot Noodle for Mark and myself. Then I had another one, as Mark wasn't hungry but I was. I was slumped and in a slump. It was the dangerous sort of low point on a trip when you take against your compadres, your willing companions. I pitched my tent under the tarp using Mark's torch again, as birds and bats whistled above.* A creature, maybe a fox, brushed by my tent but I was too tired to care. Too tired. All trolleyed out. When it began to rain I was glad I was under two layers of shelter.

The next morning, amid more rain, we rose and packed our cumbersome belongings. There was a campsite marked on the map a mile or two away and we speculated that it might have a bus stop, as it lay on the Kirkstone Pass road

---

* Luckily, having to borrow stuff reduces paranoid thinking about compadres and trusted companions.

to Windermere. A certain desperation raised the idea of a potential bus stop to the level of a mythical water hole in the desert, a village in a deserted rainforest or a gas station on Route 66 when your tank is showing empty.

This is one of the things I love about such hybrid trips as the one Mark and I were making: there were no rules and very quickly and quite easily you could get into difficulties largely of your own making. But because of a commitment to the (mainly arbitrary) goals you'd set yourself, you'd feel you had to continue despite sudden resistance, or road blocks you couldn't have foreseen. It was like putting an adventure filter on modern life and seeing it all afresh again. We could have driven from Ullswater to Windermere, we could have taken a taxi, or even the bus from the end of the lake. But by insisting on the loopy use of the trolley – 'Just to test a certain idea I have,' I said cryptically to Mark, in the best tradition of pretentious European-style travel writing – I had elevated the journey into one of drama needing resolution.

Wobbling along the rocky gravel track through the campsite, we mocked the sensible campers for paying £10 or more just to pitch their tents and use the concrete toilet block. *Suckers!* We looked at them hoping for some kind of recognition of our superior status, but it was too early and too drizzly; most were loitering inside the open flaps of their tents while brushing their teeth and looking disconsolately out on the Lake District in its most natural state, i.e. sopping wet.

I went into the campsite office and asked if there was a bus stop nearby. There was! Only 100 metres away. And the kind, smiling woman (the people who serve in Lake District campsite offices are universally very accommodating in my experience) also gave me a BUS TIMETABLE. This was, emotionally speaking, as exciting as getting a lift after nine hours of hitching, or finding that a train you had expected to have left is in fact late and you can easily catch it, or being given the keys to Dad's car with its tank full of gas, or being lent a house in the centre of Edinburgh, free, for the whole festival, or . . . anyway, you get the picture. By an intuitive tweaking of imaginative and accidental impacts, our trip had been elevated into something teetering on the brink of disaster (walking eighteen miles along a busy A-road while dragging an infernal trolley over one of the high passes of the Lake District in rain-drenched fog) – a small disaster admittedly, but one we had just averted by the kind offices of the campsite lady and the bus timetable, which I felt awfully clever for asking for and getting. It felt like I should have paid at least a fiver for it.

At the bus stop: two lads perhaps a third our age, respectful, thoughtful, studenty types, one with the excessive tallness of a growth spurt yet to be substantiated evenly in all parts of his body, the other burly and wide-shouldered with a huge rucksack, big enough to carry a dead body, albeit a rather small one, and with an eager-to-please grin. They engaged with us in loud, clear, unaffected northern accents, in a discussion of the odd fact that the bus stopped at the *same stop* on the *same side* whatever direction it was coming in, the road being so narrow. That they knew the bus routine was very reassuring to me, as every time I catch an unfamiliar bus I am assailed by the worry that it will drive by and ignore me, even if I am waiting at the correct bus stop. Very often I will step into the road moments before a bus cruises to a halt – just to add extra weight to my flagging-down gestures.

It is the same sort of micro-anxiety I get when a train is sitting at a platform and the sign says it is my train – but how do I know for sure? I usually ask someone, 'Is this the train to X?' 'I hope so,' is not my favourite answer; naturally I'd prefer a resounding yes.

I wish for a world with more signs . . . everywhere. People complain that there are already too many signs in Britain, but to me they have hardly scratched the surface. I reserve this neuroticism only for the built-up 'they' world that I have to traverse and temporarily live in, in between visits to the real world where I visit islands in lakes. In between lakes, even. For example, there should have been several signs explaining in detail the strange fact that the bus would stop at the same bus stop whatever way it was going, and there should have been signs showing where the bus stop was in relation to the campsite. (We went wrong at first, so returned to the nice woman in the campsite office, though I have to admit it was almost a pleasure to ask her again for more detailed directions.) More signs everywhere – except in the wilderness where there should rightly be *no signs at all*.

During the Second World War, signs were removed from English roads in the south in case the Germans landed, the idea being the paratrooper invaders would get lost or at least be held up a bit. After the war ended, some villages had got so used to having no signs they asked for them *not* to be replaced. They must have liked the power of knowing where they were, and how a stranger would immediately be somewhat obvious and powerless in comparison. Everything in England is a little like this, even carparks, designed for people who *already know how to use them*. Yet my whole life seems to be about doing things for the first time; as soon as I get competent at something I find myself in some new situation. The 'they' world isn't built for the likes of me, but in the wilderness or its acceptable substitutes, the playing field is level. It's a mystery and an open book to expert or novice alike.

It was a lovely, steamed-up, cosy, warm ride over the pass. I had forgotten how joyful a bus feels after strenuous walking. There is none of the trouble you get with cars – about muddying them up, or getting them wet with all your damp gear, or running out of fuel, or going wrong. You are in the womb of the municipal bus rumbling to a secure destination. Apart from the business of whether to press the red bell or not. I knew that Mark, being more laid-back and relaxed than me, would not be jittery about ringing the red bell once we arrived at Bowness-on-Windermere (called 'Rio' in Ransome's books), yet I was already thinking about exactly which stop would be optimal for our descent from the town to the lake's edge. Unfortunately, the bus was inadequately signed. It had no rolling LCD display showing each stop coming up. And there was no friendly shout from the driver nor any detailed signage within the bus. Being in such a warm and delightful fug, I didn't mind so much. But I nevertheless pressed too early. Still, we got to trundle through the town, gawking at all the natives.

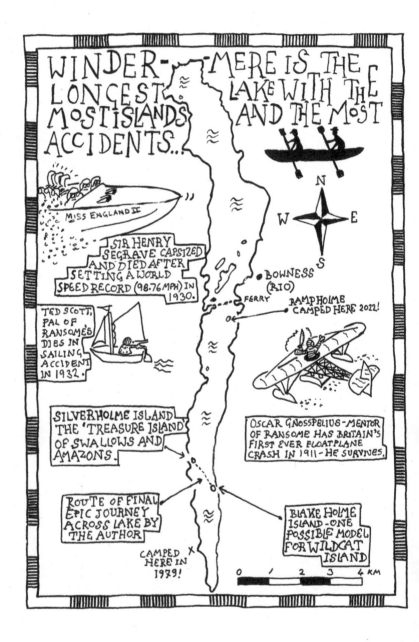

WINDER-MERE IS THE LONGEST LAKE WITH THE MOST ISLANDS AND THE MOST ACCIDENTS...

MISS ENGLAND II

SIR HENRY SEGRAVE CAPSIZED AND DIED AFTER SETTING A WORLD SPEED RECORD (98.76 MPH) IN 1930.

TED SCOTT, PAL OF RANSOME DIES IN SAILING ACCIDENT IN 1932.

BOWNESS (RIO)

FERRY

RAMP HOLME CAMPED HERE 2022!

SILVERHOLME ISLAND THE 'TREASURE ISLAND' OF SWALLOWS AND AMAZONS.

OSCAR GNOSSPELIUS - MENTOR OF RANSOME HAS BRITAIN'S FIRST EVER FLOATPLANE CRASH IN 1911 - HE SURVIVES.

ROUTE OF FINAL EPIC JOURNEY ACROSS LAKE BY THE AUTHOR

BLAKE HOLME ISLAND - ONE POSSIBLE MODEL FOR WILDCAT ISLAND

CAMPED HERE IN 1979!

N W E S

0 1 2 3 4 KM

FOUR

Wild Swans

Lake: Windermere, 64 metres deep, 18.08 kilometres long, 14.76 square kilometres
Islands: Bee Holme, Belle Isle, Crag Holme, Crow Holme, The Lilies, Lady Holme, Ramp Holme, Maiden Holme, Rough Holme

Windermere had not got the same hold as Coniston on my mind as a place of record breaking, but it attracted speed merchants as well as slow boaters like Mark and me. While not quite as myth-heavy as Donald Campbell's demise on Coniston, Henry Segrave, one of the great pioneers of water speed record breaking, died after breaking the 98mph record and then going for an extra run at an even higher speed. His powerboat, nicknamed 'the black bottomed bombshell' and officially known as *Miss England II*, hit a submerged log at 120mph, causing the boat to swerve and cartwheel into the water. It had been plagued by problems with propeller breakages and concerns about the design of the water step on which the boat planed. This step was not an integral part of the design but was bolted on and could be adjusted, yet many thought this a weakness. However, the boat was always about 'cramming a bomb into an eggshell', as Segrave put it.

Segrave was known as a true gent. I think it was this chivalrous side to record breaking that so captivated me as a boy. I appreciated the rough piratical types like Malcolm Campbell, but I had a special affection for the suave, well-mannered Englishmen of impeccable kindness and generosity who nevertheless would lay down their lives to honour a stupid bet – people such as Donald Campbell and Segrave. Before the attempt, Segrave told his keen mechanic (who was willing to work for free), 'I want you to thoroughly understand that this won't be a picnic. If anything goes wrong at the speeds we expect, no one will be left alive. I won't have anyone victimised because they are keen. How would all expenses plus £4 10/- a week do?'

'Whatever you say, sir.'

But it was not the young mechanic who would die (he escaped with light bruising), it was Segrave and his engineer. When the engineer's body was recovered two days after the crash, he was still clutching his clipboard and pencil. Segrave himself survived for three hours but died of massive lung injuries in a private house on the side of Windermere.

A long lake such as Windermere was bound to attract flying boats and in 1912 Oscar Gnosspelius, the inventor and mining engineer on whom the character 'Squashy Hat' (one of my favourites, he had specs and knew about science) is based in Ransome's novel *Pigeon Post*, successfully took off in his 40hp 'hydroplane'.* Gnosspelius ended up marrying Barbara Collingwood (who had turned down Arthur not once

---

* Incidentally, *Pigeon Post* was the first winner of the Children's 'Booker Prize', the Carnegie Medal.

but twice and is probably the model for Nancy or Peggy).[*]
Gnosspelius was really a fascinating character; he was one
of the very first to apply the lessons of the Reverend Charles
Ramus, who in his 1874 book *The Polysphenic Ship*, described
increasing the velocity a boat could go through water using a
stepped pontoon onto which the skimming boat would rise
at a certain speed. Ramus's discoveries needed the invention
of the petrol engine to really be useful, and after Gnosspelius
proved their use in his float plane, hydroplaning became
common among speedboat designers.

Author Graham Coster[†] speculates on what a brilliant
thirteenth Swallows and Amazons book it would have been
if the children had left their lake with Squashy Hat in a flying
boat rather than a sailing craft, perhaps with Captain Flint
waving at them from the stern of his houseboat?[‡] I know
that as a boy with a fascination for both float planes and the
more conventional Ransomian craft I would have loved such
a tale.

Later, Gnosspelius became one of the designers at flying
boat manufacturers Shorts, and perhaps his Lake District
connection led to their building a factory there, far from
the coast and any place obvious to German bombers. They
settled on building the giant Short Sunderland flying boat
at the north end of Windermere in enormous hangars

---

[*] The name Peggy was almost certainly inspired by the bohemian woman
called Peggy whom Ransome admired in his early days in London, who
wore long green dresses and big beads and 'met a sculptor as remarkable
as herself', leaving her civil servant husband for the artist Jacob Epstein to
begin 'a lasting partnership on a different plane of reality'.
[†] Author of interesting flying boat history *Corsairville*.
[‡] Children's book editors: I am your man to write this book.

with workers living in on-site accommodation. Thirty-five
flying boats were built; they would be towed out onto the
water when completed, miraculous huge eggs hatched into
mechanical birds that flew away. There was ample space
for taking off and landing; one even took off flying across
rather than down the lake. At the war's end, in a suitably
Sebaldian twist, this lakeside work camp was used to house
the 300 children from Theresienstadt concentration camp,
the Windermere Children I mentioned before.

Reportedly, they enjoyed their three-month stay. Some
of the outdoor activities naturally included rowing on the
lake and visiting the nearby islands at the northern end, Bee
Holme and Green Tuft.

NATIVES

There were a lot of natives that day in Bowness.* The place
was packed, as it always is, even in winter. Bowness-on-
Windermere is one of the most popular tourist spots in
the north of England. People love driving there and then
wonder why they have come. They take steamer rides and
hire rowing boats and even speedboats but almost all the
natives have that duped look, the bemused look of people
who aren't quite sure what they are doing. Which makes
them easier to ignore, overlook, consign to another, less solid,
reality.

Ransome, who, as I've mentioned, later fell out with the

---

* If you have just opened the book here, this is a technical Ransomian
term – not a derogatory one.

real-life children on which the characters of the Swallows and Amazons were based,* once mused that his inventions seemed 'solider' to him than the children who inspired them. That isn't just a novelist speaking, the same spirit is felt nebulously everywhere in the Lakes. I'm sure Wordsworth felt it when he saw the Lakes through a kind of alpine filter: the place has an insidious quality that makes you start to fantasise, reformat reality, omit uncomfortable details. And it's effortless, not like going to the South of France and trying to squint your eyes to avoid all the overcrowding and cars, all the time trying to imagine Villa La Mauresque instead of J.G. Ballard's *Super-Cannes*. The Lake District has no Eden-Olympia, no modern eyesore to bring you down, yet it is a vast and constant outdoor theatre with familiar sets all ready for a fantasy production.

INFLATION

Mark and I had a pasty at an outdoor shop and spread out with all our gear while the natives swarmed around us. We wheeled the trolley to a landing stage which was also very public and highly populous. Mark was wary of inflating the boat in such a crowd. We went through a small park to a beach covered in duck excrement. On the rocks adjoining the beach we unrolled our trusty craft. We had grown used to its slight leakage and now knew that the other two air bladders

---

* Possibly encouraged by his second wife, he believed the children were cashing in on their celebrity and obscuring his own role in actually writing the books.

were enough, in the case of a total blowout in the damaged one, of getting us to shore. Unlike the little packraft which only had one air chamber, there was something reassuring about having several. Not that I was too bothered about getting a dunking, it was the tail end of summer after all. But lakes are notoriously patchy in terms of temperature. A shallow run over one part that gets the sun can be many degrees warmer than a steep, dank drop-off in another part. And the fate of Ted Scott should always be remembered by those who take Windermere too casually.

Ted Scott was the son of the great editor of the *Manchester Guardian*, C.P. Scott, who employed Ransome as a foreign correspondent in Russia during and after the Revolution. Ted became editor himself in 1929, though he was a very different character to his father, who was an overbearing figure. Ransome had been at school with Ted and described him as his best friend (interestingly Malcolm Muggeridge, who Ransome met in Cairo and recommended him to the *Guardian*, also wrote of being 'fonder of [Ted] I think than any man I have ever come across').

Ted was introduced to sailing by Ransome. While learning to sail in the Norfolk Broads, both Ted and his son Dick had fallen in. Ted stayed with the boat but Dick swam to shore. Perhaps Arthur suspected they were jinxed or careless, because in a letter he writes: 'don't go and get drowned till I am there to fish you out!' Ted announced he wanted 'a boat like *Swallow*' and Ransome said he knew just the thing – better, in fact, as it was unsinkable because it had airtanks inside it. Then, one April day when Ted and Dick were sailing on Windermere, the boat capsized and while Dick this time clung to the upturned boat, Ted swam for the shore. His heart had threatened problems for at least two years; in fact, one of the reasons he wanted to sail was the relief it provided him from the stress of running the newspaper. On the bank he suffered a major heart attack brought on by the shock of the cold water. Ransome blamed himself doubly: first, for introducing Ted to sailing and, second, for recommending the boat. It was not, of course, his fault; there were no drysuits or even wetsuits in 1932.

And only two years before, the fictional *Swallow* had suffered a disastrous sinking in Swallowdale. Captain John had held on until the last minute before throwing the anchor and diving in to swim to shore.

And nor are we wearing wetsuits today. It's early September and warmer than April, and I am confident that should we capsize we will be able to invert the flooded canoe and bail it out with my tea mug. Ted's boat may have had airbags but ours is all airbag – light and unsinkable, bar an attack by swordfish.*

And so we paddle off. There is the usual moment of deciding who will have the double-bladed paddle and who the single. Having crossed half of Canada in an ultra-traditional birchbark canoe (made of real birchbark) and using ultra-traditional paddles, I have absolutely no qualms at all about mixing kayak double paddles with canoe single paddles. Whatever works. Doubles offer more power and control but using two sets in a small boat can lead to blade clashes. A single at the back can also be a useful rudder. But

---

* This is not as comical as it may sound. Anatoly Kulik's 2008 to 2013 Russian circumnavigation of the globe in an inflatable catamaran almost foundered when a school of swordfish repeatedly punctured both hulls. Later, a shark took a large bite out of one hull.

sometimes I like to have a change and Mark uses the single. I am always at the back; it's the driving seat.

We're going well this drizzly, misty day; the short break has given our arms, if not our legs, a rest. The rhythmic splashing of forward movement, the slight wobble as waves run our length, lifting the nose a fraction then riding underneath, the inevitable water that dribbles back up your sleeves (in a Buffalo jacket this is absorbed and hardly noticed), all the familiar experiences of paddling come back within a few strokes.

Windermere is a very different lake to Ullswater. The hills are set far back, and there is flat land, some fields, but mostly woods, coming right to the shore. There are no startling mountains near enough to really care about. And being a wide long lake, it has a loch or even sea loch quality – yes, it's easy to imagine a nasty accident on a cold spring day here.

Yet I've capsized on this lake before, many times in fact as I attempted to replicate doing what was then called an Eskimo roll on a Scout camp when I was fourteen. The camp was right down the other end of the water. There were no islands in sight but the closest would have been Silver Holme, the model for Cormorant Island in Ransome's books. The thing was, at that age, hemmed in by a rule-bound world largely of my own imagining, I assumed that any island would now be private, off-limits, hard to get to. We had canoes and we could have made an expedition to visit the islands. I don't think we even looked at them on the map.

Training to do the roll had involved a six-week course at a swimming pool in Oxford. My main memory is draining my ears afterwards. We didn't have ear plugs, or hoods on, which we complained, Eskimos* do. Scooping up all that water and having it dribble out on the bus journey home put me off rolling for life. Though I did manage to learn how to do it. So, in an excess of zeal, I did a roll on Windermere during that Scout camp and found it was surprisingly a lot easier in a long canoe than the short ones we had learnt in. But straightaway my thin 'waterproof' began to leak through and chill me. It was a case of not having the right kit. With a properly waterproof top and a hood, well, maybe I would have embraced the kayak rather than the more stately canoe, which isn't meant to be rolled (though experts can).

Today, we also both got wet pretty quickly. Getting into the canoe involved bringing in some water, which naturally wetted trousers. Paddling wetted arms, though a Buffalo top is good and warm for such damp activity. You get wet in boats and when you camp you carry that wetness with you. The weather had gone from sunny to cloudy with showers, so we needed to be careful we didn't accumulate too much damp along the way. When you're unpacking your rucksack in a wet tent while wearing wet clothes, there sometimes comes a moment of weakness when you put your dry sleeping bag down on the wet groundsheet and then get inside it in only slightly damp clothes, but over time everything becomes saturated. And if you have a down bag then it stops keeping you warm. It's a peculiarly British kind of problem. In colder countries, the water freezes and it's dry that way. In warmer countries, things dry out overnight. But in Britain, with the temperature hovering 5°C above 0, with pouring rain, you get the worst of both worlds. The Swedish explorer Mikael

---

* This was the 1970s, remember.

Strandberg (who has crossed Siberia in winter) claims the coldest he's ever been was while living in Manchester in an unheated damp house . . .

Belle Isle is the big first island that dominates your exit from Bowness. We decided to circle it, going right and taking the small island of Lady Holme first. This once had a chapel which has long disintegrated. Monks too, once lived here, with fishing rights for ten nets. Perhaps it is the fish which keep the current occupants, a colony of gulls at one end of the island and the cormorants at the other.

We saw a dog on Belle Isle but no people. It has a large eighteenth-century house and well-tended gardens, with a little motorboat for popping across the water. Being such a big and obvious island, it attracted the Roman governor of Ambleside who built a villa there and, in a historical nod to the idea of a bolthole, the island was the site of a Royalist holdout against Parliamentarians during the Civil War. The Roundheads bombarded the island from Cockshott Point,* but the King's men were able to shelter behind the dense foliage and remained unharmed. No amphibious assault is recorded. Before 1781, the island was known as Longholme, but in that year it was bought by the wealthy Curwen family, who renamed it Bella Island after their daughter Isabella. Later on, the Ordnance Survey managed to change the name to Bell Island and later Belle Island.

The distinctive round house, the construction of which began in 1784, was not popular. William Wordsworth called it 'a pepper pot' in *The Prelude*, and Dorothy Wordsworth wrote in her journal that 'one of the pleasantest spots on

---

* Presumably named after a similar unsuccessful gunnery exercise.

earth had been deformed by man. Mr Curwen's new shrub-
beries looked pitiful enough but that great house cannot be
covered. Even the tallest oaks would not reach the top of it.'
When Dorothy was invited to stay with the Curwens, she was
still not impressed. She thought the island 'dull and remote'
and wrote: 'What I like least in an island residence is being
separated from men, cattle, cottages and the goings-on of
rural life.'

Perhaps she would have been pleased from the grave that
the house burnt down in 1996 despite the valiant efforts of
over eighty firemen, who first had to cross to the island before
they could even start putting it out. A lot of the fittings and
furnishings were saved and now the house has been restored
to its former glory.

This still being an inhabited island, complete with 'No
Landing' and 'Private Property' signs, we naturally kept away.
I had thought I might want to trespass on these inhabited
islands but I felt no urge. An island with people on it is
already claimed, damaged goods. When the people leave, it
regenerates and becomes uninhabited again, virgin, welcom-
ing. It is nothing to do with the size of the island. It is to do
with the pure joy of exploration.

Ransome knows this, it's why the Swallows and the Amazons have almost nothing to do with Rio (aka Bowness) and
the big island, though marked, is simply referred to as Long
Island. To create afresh the joy of exploration, you have to be
a bit canny and places with people are harder to reimagine
than places without. And in the case of Ransome, he is reim-
agining himself as a child experiencing these adventures, so
it is with the eyes of someone who has witnessed the First
World War and the Russian Revolution that he is deliberately

creating a world of charming, nostalgic fun. The actual Swallows, when they were taken in hand by 'Uncle Arthur', soon found their boisterous ways were not appreciated. As Susan Altounyan wrote years later: 'Uncle Arthur's wrath was as explosive as his mirth and very startling to small girls.' The very first time he met the children, it was their noisiness he found most noteworthy and probably irritating (at the beginning, he was very polite in writing about his small muses, but later they would be called brats and worse . . .); and yet the children portrayed in the book are very well behaved, far more polite to each other than I was to my sisters, and serious. There is no teasing or mockery or monkeying for position. Indeed, it was really the portrayal of a late Victorian family.

This touches on a very crucial event. When Ransome was eight years old, his father, who was a professor of chemistry at York College (now Leeds University), threw him into the lake and expected him to swim by virtue of natural necessity. Arthur sank and had to be rescued. So humiliated was he in failing to come up to his loony dad's high standards, he secretly took himself off to Leeds municipal baths and taught himself to do the sidestroke. When he told his father he could now swim, he was promptly told he was 'a little liar'. This stung him so much it rings through the years and the pages, such as when John is told by Captain Flint that he's a liar.

Now, Captain Flint is also an aspect of Ransome, so the older man is channelling his father who is telling off, once again, the younger boy. But John, like Arthur, is not a liar either. (The lie he is supposed to have told involves a firework attack on Captain Flint's boat.) And we know that Ransome is channelling his own humiliation too, as the first thing John does after getting all hot and angry at the false accusation is to swim round the island. And the next thing that happens is a visit by their mother with a message from the distant naval father (who never appears since he is in fact Ransome's dead father, who died shortly after Ransome learnt to swim) in the form of a letter telling Roger he will get a penknife of his own once he can swim. Which, of course, is Ransome reworking the past, as if in a dream but with the better outcome: a gift for learning rather than a near drowning, and a determined little boy teaching himself in secret.

Swimming is a crucial skill in *Swallows and Amazons*, though one that is never needed. In Enid Blyton's stories, swimming sometimes plays a crucial role (as in the mammoth swim in *The Island of Adventure*) but the acquisition of swimming is never important. And certainly nor are lying and swimming, which were crucial to Ransome – probably even more so because of the untimely and even slightly ludicrous death of his father. The constant chopping off of bits of his infected leg are reminiscent of the running gag in Waugh's *Decline and Fall*, when a boy is shot in the foot by the starter's pistol at the school games, and then gradually dies as the infection spreads.[*]

We paddled on.

Yet I was now thinking about children's books. What kind would I write myself? (I had written one when I was twenty-four – 'Marcus Mayhem and His Magic Trainers', never published.) Would it be even *possible* to write something in the Ransome genre? Something about privately educated

---

[*] Literally a *running* gag.

middle-class kids on holiday, in, say, Scotland (taking up where Ransome ended with his twelfth Swallows and Amazons novel, *Great Northern?*). They would have to have a draconian parent or guardian who forbade the use of the internet. If they lived somewhere super-remote like Knoydart in the West Highlands it's conceivable, yes, it could be done. Or maybe they lived in Canada. Again, it would have to be very remote to work properly.

Yet my first thought was to write a series called *Survivors* (probably influenced by the TV of my youth, as apocalyptic John Wyndham-style programmes were popular and there was a show of that name). The idea would be to have four children who were surviving after a terrible pandemic or economic disaster, living perhaps on an island in the Lake District. But that would be far too serious . . .

I'm just not sure you could write about England in the Blyton or Ransome vein anymore. It's simply too suburban, too crowded. And even if you relocated to a remoter spot, there would always be a strong pressure to include an 'us and them' current. It would be like an account I read of a girl who had a very strict Mormon upbringing in Utah. It would be *weird*. Ransome is, after all, writing about his childhood, the time before the First World War when everyone thought a happy life of fishing and sailing would go on forever. Today, the Swallows would be worried about climate change and sewage overflow in the river. There is a sense of rush now, of moving towards some vaguely defined disaster (be it the singularity, global overheating, dead oceans, a viral pandemic), which explosively confronts the fact that humans have never been more numerous or lived longer at any time in history. Time's up on this super-success, which we know is shitting up the planet, making it dirty and used up, must be paid for, must be made to stop. And only an apocalyptic scenario will make us change.

Even when I was eight or nine years old, and reading Ransome avidly, I knew that my friends were not like the characters in his books; yet I too had some spiffing adventures involving rafts that sank, damming streams, and fighting a gang war with bows and arrows in our village. But I was always home for lunch and tea. I suppose my mistake is to think that life in the 1930s was really like that depicted in Ransome's books. I had little to judge them against after hearing my father's stories of growing up in Nagaland on the border of India and Burma. His yarns were even more exciting than Ransome's since they involved the Second World War, finding dead Japanese soldiers in jungle bunkers, discovering old tanks and going hunting with men who had taken the heads of opposing tribes.

So could you write a book set in the Lakes now with similar adventures involving a group of well-off children? They could go diving, fell running, caving, paddleboarding and wild swimming. They could still dodge the natives (though you'd have to think of a new name for them – the aliens or androids, maybe?). Parents would probably find them incredibly entitled and self-satisfied unless they rescued some alien kid or other who had tumbled down an old mine. They could have an uncle back from Afghanistan, former Special Forces, who knew all about survival. They could sneak onto Haweswater and live on their own secret island while dodging the evil, polluting electricity board. (There's that agenda creeping in again.) Perhaps the uncle is a birdwatcher and, indeed, like in Ransome's *Great Northern?*, the plot involves thwarting those intent on robbing nests . . .

Do children still want to read about those who go to private schools, who are wealthier and more privileged than their readers, yet who aren't snobs or cowardly or despicable in some way? I think *some* would; we all have a healthy interest in people of higher social status than ourselves. All the same, it's interesting when Anthony Horowitz created his boy spy hero Alex Rider, he had him go to a comprehensive school in his later years (even though he was very wealthy) just to 'toughen him up'.

The notion that public school children (i.e. those who go to private school) are tougher and more resilient than the state-educated is no longer a viable public myth. Often the public school kids, with their skater gear, drugs and music, desperately want to emulate their state school counterparts. Our culture has been split by the countercultural seismic shifts of the sixties and seventies and boarding school only seems to have broad appeal when it is fantasised as in Harry Potter. Fantasy again . . .

Mark and I completed our paddle around Belle Isle, taking a look at the micro-islands known as The Lilies. These were covered in lily of the valley in the past and people would row out to pick the flowers . . . which they did rather too much as there are very few of the plants left now.

A last wistful look at Belle Isle, where Ransome's Great Aunt Susan, a relative who lived in Windermere, competed in archery competitions in a green uniform of tabs and tassels. Ransome looked forward to tea with his aunt as the only relief during his time at his hated Windermere prep school. His eccentric fox-hunting and bow-wielding aunt has more than a hint of Nancy the Amazon about her.

An underwater cable cuts Windermere in half and oper-
ates the car ferry. On a later trip, when I visited Silver Holme,
the waves were too high and the ferry shut down. But today
the ferry was working full tilt, clanking and swishing its way
across the lake while we held back from it, keen not to get
caught up in the cable. While waiting for it to pass by, we
investigated Maiden Holme and Crow Holme.

Maiden Holme was tiny and quite possibly floating (it
has been moved at least once by park rangers); all it really
consists of is a tree growing out of a driftwood log. Stuck in
its branches was a pair of black swimming trunks.

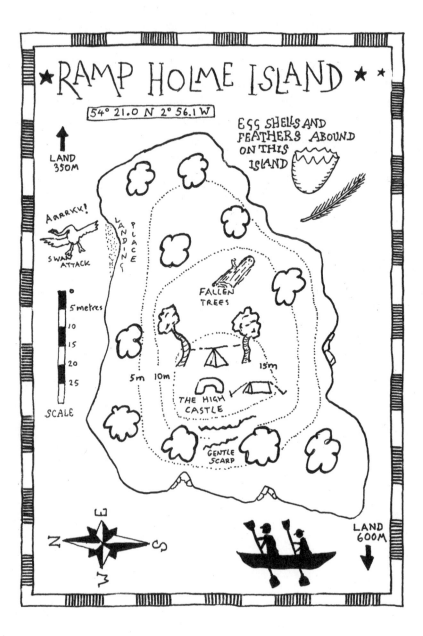

Crow Holme is an island about fifty metres long, once known as Kennel Holme owing to it being the home of the hounds of the Windermere Harriers. All long gone, along with the Oxenholme Staghounds and the Cockermouth Beagles. (The Melbreak Hounds are still going, though.) Crow Holme is a place of mushrooms and fallen trees. We found blewits, shaggy parasol and stinkhorn, along with the ubiquitous fly agaric. Crow Holme was mossy underfoot without a scrap of grass, which had been eaten by ducks no doubt. There were the ancient and collapsed remnants of what we took to be the kennels.

We paddled on through mildly turbulent waters to Ramp Holme, whose name means 'wild garlic'. This was another island you weren't supposed to camp on. A high, rocky central part had something fort-like about it and there was a handy depression hidden from outside view that was big enough for a fire and a tent. Dick Kelsall, the son of a Lake District neighbour, and whom Ransome encouraged to sail and fish, was told by Ransome that Wild Cat Island was based partly on Ramp Holme; Ransome felt the approach to it and how it looked from a distance most coincided with his image of Wild Cat. (As a young man, Dick had been a stalwart visitor to Ransome's home during the author's last illness, when he reported that reminiscences about the pleasure his stories had provided trumped any interest Ransome showed in the outside world.)

Ramp Holme had also been known as Roger Holme; it was granted by Henry VIII to Allan Bellingham, Esq., and now belongs (with the other Bellingham estates in Cumbria) to the present Earl of Suffolk. I was glad of this, assuming leniency in the policing of the isle. Owing to receiving fairly bad press over the last few centuries, aristocrats tend to be less petty than those with new money, oligarchs and utility companies when it comes to evicting middle-class interlopers. At least, that was my own reading of this tricky subject.

There were swan feathers and swan shit abounding on the island. As we landed, two swans and their cygnets came a-swimming and tried to drive us from the beach. They came steaming up and spread their wings, the dad rising up on his webbed feet like a waterskier getting going. But I was having none of it. Bullying isn't on, even by swans, and swans are natural bully boys, used to getting their own way, what with there being a royal warrant for their protection, etc. I slapped at the water with the paddle and prepared to get into a right kerfuffle, but the daddy swan backed down, as did one of the feisty younger ones. They turned tail in a rather cool manoeuvre that made it look like they'd planned to do just that all along. As they departed I loudly shared the story of my grandfather who got a hankering for a taste of swan when he was in the trenches of Ypres. After surviving the war he illegally bagged one on Cannock Chase and prepared it for a feast. 'Tasted like goose,' he'd said, sixty years later.

'They'll probably be back,' observed Mark.

'Probably. Let's hope they don't bring reinforcements.'

'Judging by the amount of shit on this island every swan must think this is home.'

'No wonder they got a bit proprietorial.'

We brought the boats inland and settled down for a brew.

I got water from the lake, which was probably a bad idea but it was what they always did in *Swallows and Amazons*. Unlike in Ullswater, a lot of sewage routinely gets dumped in Windermere – and you can blame United Utilities* for that. I was also, as I waded out in bare feet, on the lookout for leeches. Of the thirteen species of leech in the UK, ten occur in the Lake District, including the rare medicinal leech. On the eastern side of Windermere were a couple of tarns which were apparently so full of these leeches that the owners never bathed in them; medicinal leeches are the only ones that actively attack man, but I wasn't overly keen on any kind of leech.†

Back with the water, I brewed the tea and settled down for a bit of a read. Reading when you are on a trip is something you settle into after a day or two when the conversational highs of the early parts of the trip have settled down, yet you need entertainment of some kind, even something to take you away from your present idyllic surroundings you've worked so hard to get to. I took out for the nth time my dog-eared copy of *The Last Englishman*, a biography of Ransome that though excellent in its own way, treats him as a bit of a fool. The taste is ungenerous, though with a good eye for the ridiculous. What the author refuses to celebrate is Ransome's reach, his polymathic prowess. Ransome wrote on everything from fitness to modern art, from politics to fishing. In one letter, he describes penning a philosophical debate between Socrates and a homunculus. Though Ransome was a flawed

---

* Why not write and complain, sewage is not *good*.
† G.A.K. Hervey and J.A.G. Barnes (eds), *Natural History of the Lake District*, Frederick Warne and Company, 1970.

man he was self-made largely and self-educated after his
disastrous schooling. He played chess with Lenin for Chrissakes – give him some respect! This was my feeling. For the
incredible gift of his novels I forgive him his later grumpiness
to the Altounyan children, the initial muse-models for his
yarns, though it bears repeating the real models were himself
and the Collingwood sisters.

LOOKING AFAR AT AN ISLAND FOR A LONG TIME

You see an island and at first you aren't always sure it's an
island. If it's on a lake, the foliage of the shore can deceive
you very easily. Or if there's a neb or a neck or a salient of
land pushing into the lake, that can look like an island when
it isn't. But sometimes the island is obvious. Sea islands are
like that, but some lake islands too. You spot the island and
you start to make plans.

Staring from the Peak of Darien, modelled on one of the
promontories overlooking Coniston, the children in *Swallows
and Amazons* develop an overpowering urge to go to the
island. They all write letters to their father who is in Malta
but 'under orders for Hong Kong'. Titty's letter is the longest.
In it she recounts how they had seen that the lake was like
an inland sea. And in the sea was an island and of course all
four of them had been filled at once with the same idea. It
was not just an island. It was *the* island, waiting for them. It
was their island. With an island like that within sight, who
could be content to live on the mainland and sleep in a bed
at night?

And then when the adventure is over Titty sees that the island was once more the uninhabited island that she had watched for so many days from the Peak of Darien . . . Titty would think of it as Robinson Crusoe's island. It was her island more than anyone's because she had been alone on it.

The shape-shifting Ransome is Titty here (he's been Roger earlier when he says that for Roger the island would always be the place where he first swam). We know that Ransome's father gave him his own copy of *Robinson Crusoe* as a reward for reading the book cover to cover. I think I was nine or ten when I read it; it's not a hard book to read and I had already cut my teeth on the inferior and much more difficult *The Gorilla Hunters* by R.M. Ballantyne, which I had only read to impress the teacher. As I've already mentioned, what struck me about *Robinson Crusoe* was the practicality of it, the everydayness. Of course, I didn't then know that it was written as fake travelogue, and the first novel in English to establish firmly what I have always hoped of novels: that they are based on a true story. (And if they aren't based on a true story I hope they are rooted in the life of the author, that they provide a key to unlock his troubled psyche.)

Once you have seen it, you stare at the island. Ransome had been staring at the island in his mind since he had learnt to read. Then you start to make a plan. You look at the water, how it changes, what kind of boat will make it, what kind of boat you know you can handle. You make the plan. You fantasise about what you will find on the island. You search for clues. You look for a good place to land.

THE NIGHT ON RAMP HOLME

We were going to have a fire when it got dark enough, so until then we used the gas stove. I made some food and then a brew of tea for myself as Mark doesn't drink tea or coffee. As night fell the urge to build the fire dwindled. We'd been talking all day and often the fire is when you look forward to talking more but we were talked out. I had another brew and the blue–yellow hissing brightness of the stove had to stand in as a fire.

Chat faded with the light. Why did we eschew again the easy camaraderie of a fire? That ever-present feeling of eyes upon us and not wanting to attract too much attention, not wanting to be like the other trippers . . .

I tied the boats together in case the wind got up, and slept with a half paddle next to my sleeping bag. Against an intruder, I said to myself. The memory of the earlier swan escapade and Mark's casual observation that the island might be the night roost of Windermere's swan population did play across my mind.

So with a casualness that belied our concern, Mark and I retired to our tents to cogitate upon swans and get some sleep. Which I did until woken by incredible noise.

The flapping and honking of swans and quite possibly geese too.

I imagined the swans orchestrating the whole thing. Rounding up all the geese of Windermere to honk us off that island.

At night, on a lake, sound from a mile away can zoom across the water and hit your ear as if it were a few yards distant. It helps if the water is still and the wind blowing the sound in your direction. Night means there is no solar agitation of the air; that is the only difference I can think of. Get out of the sun and into shade on a winter's day and you can feel the difference.

Mark later said he thought our tents would be attacked by the angry birds.

'You know you're losing it when you're googling "wild swans" and "do swans attack humans?" at one in the morning,' he wryly admitted the next day. But I knew what he meant; the cackling and flapping had been most disconcerting.

They may simply have been honking all around the shore and only seemed close by. In any event, it was a loud night, a night of spoilt dreams and lying awake, fretful and alert – but on a trip you expect to sleep badly and it doesn't seem to spoil the following day.

Now it was all about leaving and getting back to shore. We passed Chicken Rock and Hen Rock on the way back – bird roosts rather than islands. Mark had to head home and I had to continue alone to Coniston and to the ultimate destination of my trip: Wild Cat Island.

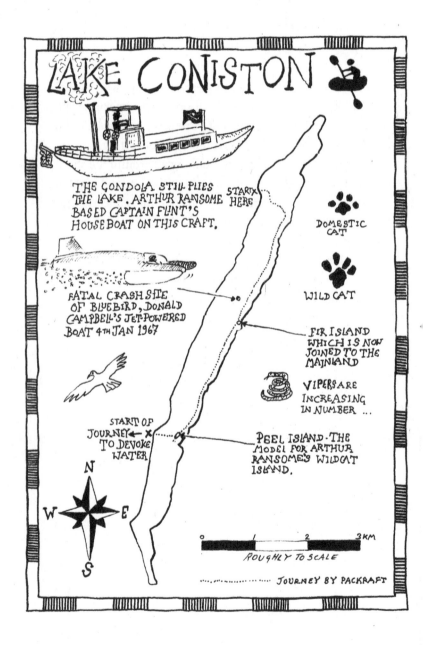

LAKE CONISTON

THE GONDOLA STILL PLIES THE LAKE. ARTHUR RANSOME BASED CAPTAIN FLINT'S HOUSEBOAT ON THIS CRAFT.

START HERE

DOMESTIC CAT

WILD CAT

FATAL CRASH SITE OF BLUEBIRD, DONALD CAMPBELL'S JET-POWERED BOAT 4th JAN 1967

FIR ISLAND WHICH IS NOW JOINED TO THE MAINLAND

VIPERS ARE INCREASING IN NUMBER ...

START OF JOURNEY ← X TO DEVOKE WATER

PEEL ISLAND · THE MODEL FOR ARTHUR RANSOME'S WILDCAT ISLAND.

N
W E
S

0   1   2   3 KM

ROUGHLY TO SCALE

·············· JOURNEY BY PACKRAFT

FIVE

To Wild Cat Island

Lake: Coniston, 56.1 metres deep, 8.8 kilometres long,
4.91 square kilometres
Islands: Peel Island, Fir Island

It was arguably the key moment of the entire trip and yet I
didn't know where to park my car. It had valuable kit inside,
mainly my laptop with all my writing that I foolishly had never
backed up, but which I was taking with me to Wigtown Book
Festival after my exploration of Coniston and the little-known
Devoke Water. I needed a safe place for my car, yet I didn't
know of any in the Lake District, not offhand anyway. They
are even planning to ban tourist cars from the Lake District,
which would obviously be a great idea (I love the idea of those
rip-off carparks with cameras and lights going bust), but I
didn't want them to ban parking when I was still there with
my car. I thought about leaving it by the road, maybe in a
lay-by on a remote road, but I was not brave enough. I asked
at YHA Hawkshead if I could leave it in their carpark – but no
dice. In the end, the very helpful and nicely situated Coniston
Hall campsite let me leave my car there for five pounds a day,
which seemed like a bargain for peace of mind.

I parked next to another tent. Not near to it, at least thirty metres away, but because the campsite was vast and almost empty, it looked like I had chosen to park near them, when actually I had selected this spot because I wanted my car to be shaded under trees. When the owners of the tent came back in their car, they started making comments as they pottered around, such as, 'Come a bit closer, why don't you?' And then, as I was getting changed into my canoeing gear, 'Put a top on, for God's sake.' Feeling paranoid, I looked across and saw that they were getting changed too. These comments were just overheard banter but like the noise of the swans the night before, the sound was travelling further than you might imagine. The banterers walked past and were loudly and politely friendly. I had thought them two lads in their twenties judging by their snazzy, souped-up Honda, but they were at least in their forties and just having a laff, though a bit aimless too, walking to the village at 4 p.m. or so, a bit early for the pub.

This time, I would be packrafting as hiking would follow my exploration of Coniston. I was looking forward to it. My pack was heavy but bearable. The raft weighed only 1.5 kilos, if you recall, and only the paddles were too heavy really for this kind of lark. My original plan had been to fashion thin plywood or plastic paddle blades with 'U' bolts that fixed them to my walking poles, which would be strapped together in the middle with a strip of sliced inner-tube rubber (a great multi-purpose binding). But I had not done this, so I was stuck with my big, old, demountable yet in truth rather heavy kayak blades. Looking at islands, staring at islands as we passed them on Windermere and mentally picturing myself in the tiny packraft had convinced me that proper paddles were needed. With a single-bladed micro-paddle (as some packrafters use) I'd be left spinning in circles.

For the packraft, really, is the inflatable descendant of the coracle, that peculiarly English craft. (Irish coracles, called curraghs, are more streamlined and boat-like than the cockleshell coracle.) In a coracle – and I had made one when I was thirteen – you have to paddle quickly on one side and then on the other if doing it the traditional way with a single paddle. Of course, you can use a pole, which is very effective in some kinds of river. But the coracle is really meant for floating downstream, and you pick it up and carry it when there is any obstruction.

The packraft was my friend, the packraft was my toy. Dearly I loved that packraft and fettled it like it was something special and shiny, instead of being a rum, old piece of plastic or specially treated nylon or whatever those darn clever folks over in the United States of Phlegmerika do to make these darned clever outdoor toys for folks such as my good self, who are wedded most seriously to an idealised post-childhood concept of mucking about in the woods and the water. Really, all we outdoor adventure folks are doing is reliving our idyllic childhoods and recruiting people who didn't have such childhoods, but are now imagining what it would have been like. Because childhood is the only place where you can really be free. Free to do what you like and free from the worry of the impending end of the world.

My generation came of age with the threat of the bomb hanging over us. Going to see the Peter Watkins film *The War Game*, which is compiled very cleverly from Second World War footage of Dresden and Coventry intercut with scenes of horrific hopelessness, turned me into a youthful peace protester. The boss of Sun Microsystems suggested that nanotechnology would end the world and I believed that too for a while. Today, in the most extreme version of global warming we have the deadly threat of a methane belch from the melting subarctic tundra, something so devastating that we'll all be consumed in the fires of a proto-Venusian summer. But not quite yet. Somehow we must get on with living and enjoying this beautiful world. While it lasts.

The packraft was ritually inflated using the big red bag. How I loved that big red bag! It was yet another example of true Yankee genius, that bag. Every other darn sucker in the inflatable business uses standard valves and standard pumps. Who wants to lug a pump in the wilderness? Not I, no, siree! Not I! No, the true Yankee geniuses (there must be more than one) at Alpacka, the inventors of the modern packraft, came up with the big red bag which fills the packraft indecently fast. Indecently, because for anyone used to inflatable-this-that-and-the-others – from rubber rings to bouncy castles – the concept of boredom and inflating go hand in hand. You pump and pump for what seems like far too long and still the damn thing is as limp as a wrung-out dishcloth. Then, suddenly, it is pretty much inflated. The last tenth of pumping time is what supplies the high pressure; the preceding nine tenths are just about shifting bulky amounts of air – which the big red bag does brilliantly.

Then, with my packraft on the gravel beach of Coniston and no one else about, I blew into the 'top-up valve' and made it drum tight and ready for adventure.

I had with me my favourite well-tested rucksack of yore, meaning the one used on my last big walk: an Osprey, a brand of reliability and ingenuity but of only average looks. This one, black and orange, looked inspired by trainer design and I had cut off many superfluous buckles, belts and water-bladder supports to make it about 200 grams lighter. Never once have I missed any of the cut-off bits. Water bladders are a particularly useless item; you can't properly wash them out like you can a Nalgene bottle and they encourage sipping like a dowager as you march along with a standpipe in your mouth, sip, sip, sip. Water, as every born survivor knows, must be consumed in calm, cool conditions before a hike or in the evening after it. Perhaps at midday if the weather is hot but only when resting. Sip while sweating at your peril. Oh, I know marathon runners and the like sip all day long but their game is different. For them, water is acting as a coolant – in and out, carrying plenty of salts with it. The walker aims to reduce sweating to a minimum. And the paddler too, come to think of it.

This rucksack had endeared itself to me by virtue of its rip-proof exterior and the gap between my back and the back of the rucksack – a handy space for swirling, cooling air. The old Karrimor pack frames allowed for this better than any kind of modern sack, and I'd been tempted to use one again; certainly, it would rest better on the front of the packraft and leave more space for my feet.

For this was going to be the problem, I foresaw, as I waded out on the shallow, flat, grey, pebbly beach – a sunny beach, the lake steamer chugging by in the distance, full of lovely old grandmas and grandads, families, small waving kids, everyone we were anxious to leave behind. This would be the problem: pack too vast for tiny raft.

Crammed up the fat end of the boat (mentioned already,

but just a reminder that packrafts are asymmetric in design with a bolstered rear end to balance your butt weight), I gingerly laid down my pack. Its attractive curved back design (not really necessary but it looked 'cool') with wingy-tip-type hip extensions was awkward to accommodate at the front. Laid flat, the hip extensions touched the water; the other way up, it wobbled. In the end, I sort of half leant it, half stood it up in the bows and wedged my feet in, legs bent, a definitely cramp-inducing posture.

I skidded myself off the grey, pebbly bottom, trusting in the sturdy floor of the packraft, which is even stronger than its air-bladder sides. I had under my arse my Therm-a-Rest,* which was the exact size of the bottom of the boat; Alpacka had designed it that way, I'd heard. It was very pleasing to use one bit of kit for another use, even if it was simply to keep my nether quarters warm in the long passage down chilly Coniston. There was no extra benefit in having an inflatable bottom to the boat, and it did raise my centre of gravity, but I found the additional space between me and the watery depths, which had claimed not a few people in the past, comforting, yes, comforting indeed.

Coniston was a place of wrecks and disaster. There was the 1967 crash dive by Donald Campbell, but long before that Arthur Ransome had himself half wrecked a boat on the rocks that guard the entrance to Peel Island – my destination that day and the symbolic and emotional model for Wild Cat Island, even if other islands fill in some of the details required by the stories.

---

* The original, simplest and best sleeping mat for backpacking.

Item#1: Ransome's parents were engaged to be wed on Peel Island. Exchanged rings there.

Item#2: Peel Island was the Ransome family's favourite spot for Lakeland picnics.

Item#3: Peel Island was where Ransome met W.G. Collingwood and his artistic and literary family, and where 'his real life' began. Collingwood was the author of the Lakeland novel *Thorstein of the Mere*, one of Ransome's favourite childhood books.* This was where he decided to become a writer.

Item#4: Peel Island was where he corrected the proofs of his book on Poe, his first 'real' book. Ursula Collingwood, younger sister of Barbara, swam out to the island carrying the proofs on her head.

Item#5: Ransome always referred to Peel Island as 'our island'.

Item#6: It was here that Ransome almost wrecked a sailing boat on the rocks and, half sinking the thing, managed to bail it out, using a bootlace to fix the gaff, before getting just enough wind in the sails to break clear of what he knew would be total disaster on the sharp dentition of rock that

---

* *Thorstein of the Mere* is about a Viking lad who lives at Greenodd on the river below Windermere. A rollicking good yarn, it inspired both Ransome and Tolkien. There is definitely something of *Thorstein* in the mountains and lakes of *The Hobbit*. Ransome would later chide Tolkien for using the word 'man' from time to time when describing his hobbit. AR liked consistency.

guarded the Secret Harbour of Peel Island, an event that inspired the accident he described in *Swallowdale*.

Item#7: On his desk in Russia, Arthur had two pictures of the Lake District, a mixed collection of Russian dolls, an icon of Saint Nicholas the Miracle Worker and a sprig of heather from Peel Island.

The Secret Harbour – I had seen pictures, but what would it really be like? I was eager to find out as I made the first plippy-ploppy paddle strokes free of the shore. The lake was rippled by very light wind, the sky blue, perfect weather. But with my pack balanced a bit high the little raft felt unstable, rather like being on a bicycle with the saddle too high, or being on a bucking bronco machine that has been switched from level 1 to level 3 (with 10 being flung off over the top of the nearby bar). A bit unstable, not 100 per cent confidence-inducing. I paddled on, keeping an eye out for rogue waves.

Rogue waves! They do happen, quite mundanely and fairly often, when two waves or even three come together in accidental sync and then double or treble up as if by magic. Or when a normal pattern of waves has an anomalous little dance just off your bow and the off-rhythm battering you get topples you over. I knew enough to know that you had to keep an eye out for oddities in the waves and steer the boat accordingly. Rather like finding a delicate path that allows sideways travel across an unfeasibly steep slope, it was possible I knew from experience to paddle ferocious waters by steering a delicate course around nasty waves and wave explosions.

Though the packraft was an inelegant bumboat for serious lake work, I made progress without becoming too tired. It was slow, but not so slow as to be dispiriting. I decided to cross the lake while I had the chance, and to risk capsizing far from shore but still in good light, rather than try later when I was opposite Peel Island. Crossing wide water is like inflating a canoe (without the big red bag). You get nowhere for ages and then suddenly the far bank is coming closer quite fast and you're there.

ALL IS QUIET ON THE FAR SHORE, SAVE FOR THE SOUND, DISTANT BUT CLEAR, OF A WOODPECKER.

THE LONG HAUL UP* THE LAKE BEGINS TO TAKE ITS TOLL. THE FIRST BLISTERS APPEAR.

*CONISTON IS 5 MILES LONG.

THE FIRST SIGHT OF AN ISLAND LONG SOUGHT IS TRULY AN EXCITING FEELING... THE NEXT THOUGHT: WILL IT BE UNINHABITED?

OT-OH: PADDLE BOARDERS! THE SCOURGE OF THE HIGH SEAS! SCUM! PIRA-TICAL SCUM!

THESE ROCKS WERE MENTIONED IN THE BOOK. AND IS THAT THE LANDING PLACE I READ ABOUT AGE 9?

IT IS! GET ASHORE ME HEARTIES NEVER MIND THOSE PADDLE-BOARDERS IT IS TIME FOR A BREW AND A BIT OF EXPLORING!

Scroar! A Typhoon jet fighter fractured the skies, two white lines scratching like nails on a blue-sky blackboard. The plane is low, the pilot almost visible. I could wave like a hi-tech version of *The Railway Children*. Except there is deep nostalgia in these jets, which I remember as being far commoner when I was a child and they looked almost the same too. Jets evolved into a mature technology by about 1955 . . . sixty-five plus years ago. No wonder I feel they are somehow unmodern. Now, a large drone turbojet like the Reaper with its dead, pilotless bulge – that would be a sight . . .

Then it's quiet again as I head down the far shore for the first of Coniston's islands, Fir Island. I bumble round the small bays and inlets of the eastern shore, knowing them to be the very places that the Swallows and Amazons sailed past. Indeed, this stretch of the shore – seventeen acres of it, not including Fir Island – were bought by Arthur Ransome in 1940, an escape north from the turmoil of war. Along this very stretch of heavily wooded foreshore he walked, shot the odd fox, watched birds and was generally very grateful for being so near to his beloved Coniston. The happiness of childhood, fractured, bent, diffracted by the century, had never left him.

I kept looking out for an island when all of a sudden I was upon one – and it was Fir Island but it was an island no more! Joined by rafted-up logs and mud to the mainland, and very substantially joined too; without serious JCB work, Fir Island would soon be just another kneb, knob, point or peak, its glorious islandness lost forever.* How individual is an island? How we look at it, examine it, anticipate with eagerness the landing and exploring of it, and how disappointing it is to find it had become . . . just land. The mainland is only interesting in as much as it is a starting point for journeys to islands. In fact, I make so bold as to suggest that all the very interesting people on this planet are island people. I may be wrong here but at least have a think about it.

The island that is no more: I didn't even get out of the craft to survey it. A few pines, a mossy, needly floor, enough room for a fire and even a tent or two, but no reason ever to go there. When an island ceases to be an island, it is like a man who was once intent on a life as an artist becoming a civil servant or a lab technician or salesman of photocopying machines – all noble mainland occupations but not islands, not something you'd set sail for.

I paddled on, worried even after checking my trusty map, secure in its see-through, somewhat soft and mouldable, plastic Eurohike cover. Eurohike make cheap gear, but some of it is good – and I like the name and its faraway reminder of Interrailing, crossing Europe on a fiver a day, sleeping on beaches and arriving in Istanbul on the dawn train from Thessaloniki. I suppose all my solitary travels are an attempt to replicate in some way the excitement of the early travelling I did around Europe when I feared not a bit crashing anywhere – from a butt-strewn Milan station floor to a town square in Corfu. Well, now I am intent on

---

* Ransome writes in one letter about the irritating efforts of some Sea Scouts to connect an island on Windermere to the shore. Perhaps de-islanding islands is a mob instinct akin to lynching or looting PC World, whereas islanding is a pure celebration of the better part of being oneself?

approaching somewhere I could have visited anytime in the last forty years and haven't. And whatever signage adorns Wild Cat Island, whatever threats of a 'ranger visit', I am going to camp there.

THE GONDOLA

Steaming past as I fulfil my brief survey of what remains of Fir Island was the SY (steam yacht) *Gondola*, a small and ancient steamship that plies daily the waters of Coniston roughly north–south. Trippers lined the windows, yet my usual suspicion and scorn fails to materialise because this is both a genuine 1859 steamship, and, more excitingly, the model for Captain Flint's houseboat, which is the locus for much of the action of *Swallows and Amazons*. (There exists a postcard of the *Gondola* in the Ransome archives with a pirate flag drawn flying from its bow; with very few changes it becomes Flint's houseboat.) Another ship called the *Esperance* also had some bearing on the final design, though, as I have mentioned before, since *Swallows and Amazons* is best understood as a nostalgic rerun of his own childhood on Coniston, the *Gondola* remains the psychological model for the houseboat, as its patient chugging up and down the lake must have lodged firmly in Ransome's memory.

In general, steamships are treated dismissively in all of Ransome's books – 'sail's the thing' – and when reading these books I took on board this prejudice without question. It seemed obvious to me, growing up in the 1970s, that the world of the 1930s portrayed by Ransome (which I now know was really the 1900s) was far superior in every respect to the modern world. I seemed to have been born with a deep contempt for the present age. I cannot help it, though of course when I have some new medical treatment or other, or acquire something as useful as the packraft, I think of this in a different light to the rest of the offerings of the modern world. I refuse to see it as part and parcel of the same thing – of how you can't have the medical advance without the pollution of our small rivers and the crowding of the Lake District carparks with camper wagons . . .

And unpicking this nostalgia has little logic to it. For me, earlier periods – say the Viking era of *Thorstein of the Mere*, or the highly polluted time of nineteenth-century lead mining in the Lake District – also have little appeal. I am wedded to a romantic vision of a non-industrialised, or highly contained form of industrialisation, limited to steam trains and steamboats like the *Gondola*.

Why should steam be OK and diesel and electric be wrong? Well, steam doesn't need oil or gas to feed it, nor the whole mysterious infrastructure of extraction that makes fossil fuels so unattractive. Steam is simple and visible; you can even use wood instead of coal (or mummies, which were once burnt in steam trains on the Luxor–Cairo railway). The twentieth century is the century of the invisible: electrons we cannot see, nuclear reactions we can only observe in their effects, planets we only know about through radio telescopes. In the twentieth century, man succumbed to the ineluctable logic of reductionism, and bet the ranch on his discovery of more and more particles and events that even his most powerful microscopes couldn't observe. It seemed that this approach almost reluctantly discovered that nothing but energy was at the heart of everything, but of course this

nothingness could only be inferred since it was too small
to be seen directly. And since science has the hegemony on
reality, reality became invisible – by which I mean it favours
theoretical explanations. No wonder there is no need for
invisible realms called heaven or hell; the ultimate reality for
modern life is entirely hidden and taken on trust by all of us.

It is this reliance on the scientific invisible which has dis-
placed the real invisible, the subtle and mysterious wonders
of the natural world experienced first-hand. Just compare a
nineteenth-century nature guide to the dry and unreadable
Collins New Naturalist *Lake District* guide of the twenty-first
century. Compare the 1904 edition of *Wayside and Woodland
Trees* with the 1964 edition (which is still much better than
any current tree guide but much reduced compared to the
earlier one, based as it is on the masterful 1662 *Sylva* by John
Evelyn). The old-time naturalists spent hours just watching
and recording and talking to others who really knew about
wildlife – the hunters, farmers, poachers and vagabonds.
They have a deep humility in the face of Mother Nature;
science here lies in precise description, not in theorising,
structuring and labelling. *Let it be known that everything I
have done has more or less been a counterinsurgency against
the tame and tedious encroachment of modernity . . .*

Steam isn't boring like motorways chock-full of cars.
Steam is full of promise and though polluting, it doesn't
seem half as bad as the noxious exhaust gases of cars, lorries and jet planes. I fully understand the attractions of the
steampunk aesthetic: invention and ingenuity without the
tedium of electronics that no one can really understand. And
by 'understand', I mean visualise, since the form of understanding you need for modern physics is one of patterns and

signifiers within a system; something that only becomes false when you try to paint a picture of it. And pictures and stories are what we live by. So we inevitably create false pictures and false narratives to explain science to ourselves.

Or is it simply wanting life to resemble a story book? Ransome famously translated Russian folk tales and then created his own imaginary world of perfect childhood. Enid Blyton does the same; and by swallowing this whole as a child, and then attempting in some way to relive it, am I simply someone stranded in an idyllic vision, on my own imaginary island, imaginary as any revolutionary's image of a future perfect state? If I am, at least my island has no gulag, no civil wars, no destruction of nature . . .

The *Gondola* cost 1,000 guineas to build (in modern money, the equivalent is estimated to be about £120,000), which is probably less than it would cost to build today. It was loosely based on a Venetian gondola but was much larger at eighty-six feet long, with a screw propeller somewhat in advance of its time. The engine borrows from the latest development in railway steam engines. She plied the waters faithfully until retirement in 1936, when, as if fulfilling Ransome's imagination, she was converted to a houseboat by a wealthy grocer from Barrow. Ruined and sunk by the 1970s, she was saved by a local worthy from the National Trust and relaunched again in 1980.

And who wouldn't prefer a trip in such a wonderful relic that is nevertheless entirely suited to its task, more suited than a modern boat of some spurious design? It is a prime example of technology reaching its optimum state, and being potentially disfigured by later developments. A table is just such a piece of mature technology. Though one can imagine a 'smart table' (perhaps it tips up and deposits crumbs on the floor?), it would be ludicrous. The notion of 'progress', which is so injurious to our appreciation of the cyclical nature of things and the fact that some things mature and really cannot be improved on, nor should be, is of course allied to the nature of hypercapitalism: the need to make breakable, temporary, slightly unsatisfying things in order to drive up consumption. And look where that has got us . . .

THE NAMING OF THINGS

One aspect of Ransome's books I have yet to emulate is the naming of things. When I was a boy, I explored the neighbourhood and bestowed workaday names to places: Dump Wood (it had a dump in it), Pigeon Poacher's Wood (lots of spent 12-bore cartridges and lots of pigeons), Compass Island of course (not sure why, maybe because my compass didn't work there and it reminded me of Enid Blyton's books, which often featured places of geomagnetic anomaly and all the attendant possibilities for getting lost – a strand gone forever in the age of phone GPS). Not that I minded the grandiose names Ransome bestowed: Rio, Darien, even Wild Cat Island, I only drew the line when Dick and Dorothea referred to one place as Mars, which was too fanciful for me.

I sometimes think I should be naming things instead of looking up the correct name in a book that I only own in order to look up the correct name, and, sadly but usually, forget as soon as I have pronounced it to whoever I am informing, even when this is only me. Once I set myself the task of learning the names of all the indigenous trees of Great Britain (there are only thirty-five or so, depending on which list you agree with) and that was not too difficult. You really do see more varieties when you know their names, as you look more closely at leaf shape and bark patterns, so you look more closely at everything – which is really the main thing. I began to think that by giving a name of your own to a plant or tree – breaking off a leaf and a bit of bark and a twig and a flower and perhaps drawing a sketch of it, and then giving it a name such as Fezziwig flower or Rumpelstiltskin tree or Maradona bloom or Splukin or Nutrobe or Dryfell or whatever name took your fancy – you would be getting what you needed, which was looking more closely at the thing itself. Because the only benefit of being interested in nature is that you look more closely at 'nature' and get far more out of being alive than someone trapped in their own head all the time.

The great American artist Dan Price writes in his book *The Moonlight Chronicles* about drawing the things you see but making up their names, or even leaving them nameless – there's an idea. It's not that I am against guides – they are, after all, pretty useful in many ways – it's just that I would like to have a guide to the birds of Britain in which all the birds are described and drawn and their habits noted, but they would have new, made-up names given to them by an ornithologist who had never read another bird book . . .

The internet, as usual, has played a role. Now you just point your phone at a flower and it tells you what kind it is. In the old days you'd be lugging that Collins Guide miles just to get the same satisfaction. You earnt names in the past. But now names, like Wiki-derived factoids, are just too easy.

Once, after all, there were no names of anything. Once we were wild, free, murderous . . .

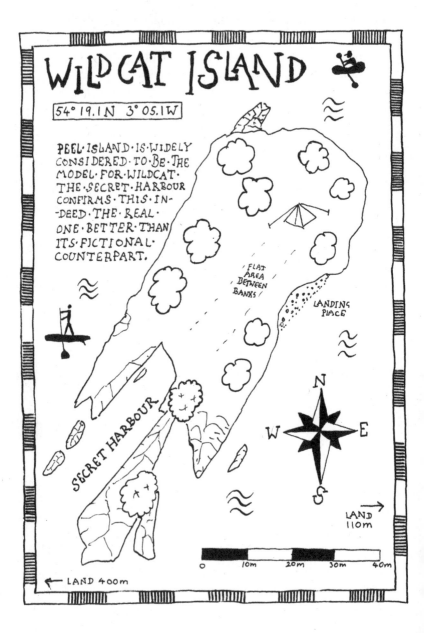

WILDCAT ISLAND

54° 19.1 N   3° 05.1 W

PEEL·ISLAND·IS·WIDELY·
CONSIDERED·TO·BE·THE·
MODEL·FOR·WILDCAT·
THE·SECRET·HARBOUR·
CONFIRMS·THIS·IN-
-DEED·THE·REAL·
ONE·BETTER·THAN·
ITS·FICTIONAL·
COUNTERPART.

FLAT
AREA
BETWEEN
BANKS

LANDING
PLACE

SECRET HARBOUR

N
W   E
S

LAND
110m

LAND 400m

0   10m   20m   30m   40m

APPROACHING THE ISLAND

It is getting late, well, later. If I don't see Peel aka Wild Cat Island before 5 p.m. maybe I should wait and camp on the bank. But then I am drawn on by the image of the 'leading lights' hung by John on the trees of the Secret Harbour as a way to approach the island at night. The concept of leading lights was one I found very exciting as a boy. One lamp is hung on one tree and another is hung a bit lower on a tree behind it. When the lights are lined up, one above the other seen from a distance, it means the trees are lined up and that is a safe line to proceed in on.

When I spot something that could be the island, I'm not sure at first. The foliage of the next curve of the bay merges with the island so well, it is hard to see if it is joined or not to the mainland. It isn't! A surge of renewed enthusiasm powers the yellow and black buzzy-bee bumboat across the water towards the sacred isle. One of the oddest things about the plethora of fan material that revolves around the Ransome corpus is the lack of emotion among the enthusiasts. For example, I just read an article in which someone pointed out that the number of windows in Flint's houseboat were fewer than those of the *Gondola*. What flatfooted nonsense! Where is thy passion, oh believer? That which soars above the mundane to see the fantasy so clearly?

The rocks at the southern end are just as described in the book, but wait, there are people there! A couple of paddleboards are visible pulled up on rocks. Interlopers.

I circle slowly and glimpse the channel that must be the Secret Harbour. Circling further, I find the landing place, a gravelly beach, the very same as the one that the Swallows and Amazons land on.

The boat is pulled up and I divest myself of wet gear on an upended root plate of a big tree; stove on, brew on, I make my base camp on the beach. A sign fixed to the rocky wall reads no camping, no fires, no overnight stays . . .

Up a steep path and over the slight lip and down into the central runnel of the island. A good five feet lower than two wooded banks either side, this central gully has gravel and closely worn grass underfoot. This is the area that was excavated by W.G. Collingwood and where he claimed to find remains of early Viking settlers in the Lake District. He used this in his novel *Thorstein of the Mere* and a passage in the book describes Peel Island. In the same book, an episode that stands out is when Thorstein saves Raineach (an early Nancy Blackett figure) from an attacking wildcat. As Ransome knew and loved the book, perhaps there is some sort of connection.

The excavated runnel is perfect for pitching tents. The island is a little smaller than the fictional Wild Cat, which has more space for camping. At the north end is a good point for looking out; the lighthouse tree, though, is gone. Darn, there are heads moving through the underbrush of the right-hand, less-visited side of the island. The paddleboard people are still about. I can wait.

When it is getting towards dusk I shift my camp to the middle of the island. The banks either side mean I am invisible. I could have a fire but I don't; most of the spare wood has been burnt already, besides which I have the comforting blue glow of my gaslighter to console me. This is my best bit of new kit: a sort of mini-blowlamp that jets pure flame in a roaring blade of blue heat. I only have to direct it in the vague direction of the gas on the stove and, *badoom*, we're alight.

From where I am sitting in the tent entrance, looking down from a height of maybe thirty or more feet along the dark length of the lake, the sky ribboned in layers of blue-grey cloud and clean stripes of utter blueness, the perspective means the surface of the water seems flat calm. Perhaps it is. There is a deep pervading calm everywhere, within and without.

Ah, Wild Cat Island, I have arrived at last.

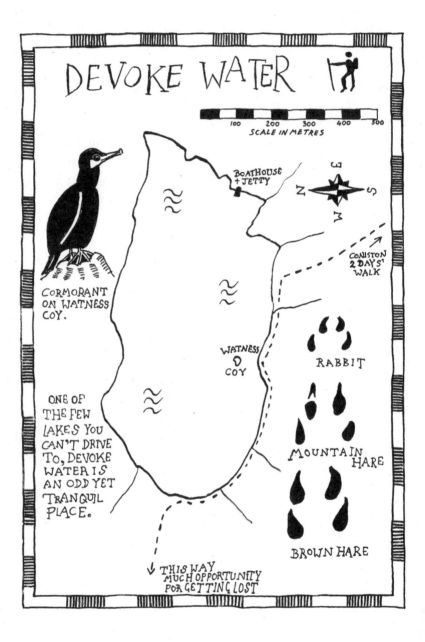

DEVOKE WATER

SCALE IN METRES
100   200   300   400   500

BOATHOUSE + JETTY

N E S W

CONISTON 2 DAYS' WALK

WATNESS COY

CORMORANT ON WATNESS COY.

ONE OF THE FEW LAKES YOU CAN'T DRIVE TO, DEVOKE WATER IS AN ODD YET TRANQUIL PLACE.

RABBIT

MOUNTAIN HARE

BROWN HARE

↓ THIS WAY MUCH OPPORTUNITY FOR GETTING LOST

SIX

Dobby Was Here

'People interested in revolutions and revolutionaries will be shocked at my not being a revolutionary, and will not understand how one with a front seat at a revolution could be always thinking of books, and worst of all, books for children.'
Arthur Ransome, letter, 1949

Lake: Devoke Water, 14 metres deep, 1.21 kilometres long, 0.52 square kilometres
Island: Watness Coy

The next lake island was to be found on Devoke Water, a little-visited lake on the western edge of the Lake District. In the single page that Wordsworth devotes to the islands of the Lake District he mentions Watness Coy, the island on Devoke, which is odd considering how obscure it is. In order to get there I needed to walk, humping my boat and paddles with me. I thought it would take two days, being realistic.

It had been a grand night to be sure, alone on Peel Island, and I was full of the early morning pleasure of it as I topped up the air in the packraft for the paddle away and across the lake. Midstream, a paddleboarder sighted me and came cruising near the island; he hove in next to me on the gravel and pebble shore. Before he could speak, the silence was fractured by the distinct sound of an over-revving engine, a boy racer on the road hidden by trees on the near bank.

'Cars,' I said, 'Even here.'

'Spoils the serenity,' said the paddleboarder. Then a pause, and cautious: 'Did you camp here?'

Bolstered by the experience, I spilled the truth. 'Childhood dream. Had to do it,' I said.

'Brilliant!' he said and I loved him as he tubgutted off on his wobbleboard.* Not for the first time, I am forced to conclude that the real people *love* renegade campers.

The lake was narrower here, at its southern end. I came clear up the bank of Coniston on a rocky, blocky shore near enough to the road for it to tempt picnicking and the inevitable dispersal of screwed-up small tissues. I kept closer to the water, which had a shine on it from the sun and was flat as a clouded, mysterious mirror. On a rock, someone had scratched quite deeply 'Dobby Was Here'. Looking at my undies drying on the boat and my wet socks on another couple of sunlit rocks: yes, he was.

All told, it took a while to pack up everything, but I was keen to be going on and doing some walking instead of paddling. I walked along the busy lakeside road for a short while, then headed up into the hills on a well-paved side road wending steeply in the morning sunshine through bracken and scrubland forest on either side, and with sheep grazing negligently on the road, there being no fences. The sheep I

---

* This sentence contains made-up words intended to convey obesity.

swore at, as is my custom, 'You couple of buggers,' I said in a not unfriendly tone. Whenever I see cows and sheep and pigs and such like, I tend to swear and speak to them in a way that would not be allowed to a fellow human in these equitable times; indeed, I speak to them as an evil master to his much put-upon servant. I do so without, of course, expecting any kind of response or action; it is simply for the pure pleasure of a sort of S/M interaction denied those who are not indulging that side of their personality elsewhere. I can safely say that no steer, porker or dullard ewe has ever butted me for such rudeness and apart from the loathsome content of my comments, there is no underlying aggression or hostility per se; but you never know what the future holds as animals gain even more rights year on year – and probably rightly so, given how shamefully they have been treated by modern farmers on factory farms, etc.

Also a certain loneliness – no, the wrong word – *a certain feeling of not having spoken a single word for too long* can overcome one in the absence of a fellow walker's ear to bend. I made do with the sheep. No doubt the excuse of many a poor fool. But hey up, hadn't I spoken to the lardy paddleboarder earlier on? In my defence, I suppose I had not spoken *in an uninhibited way* for a long time, all interactions with stray humans being strictly under control in case I said the wrong thing, gave offence, gave the game away, was arrested for being a wild camper, etc., etc.

The little tarmac road through the bracken wilds got very steep indeed, in the way that little roads do and big roads do not. A big road needs wide bends and if too steep it cannot bend. Think making a spiral with a string versus a noodle float. If that helps. Anyway, the heat was on me now and I was fair sweating up that steep road, so I began to sing a deliberately tuneless song and in between verses I felt some eyes upon me. I turned to find an electric Toyota SUV right up my arse with its vast grinning grille and bug-eyed lights and almost total silence. Shock mingled with a certain gratitude that the driver (hidden in the modern cowardly way behind smoked glass) had resisted the urge to toot the horn to get me out of the middle of the admittedly very narrow road. Imagine if he or indeed she had tooted: the middle of nowhere, not a car in sight, right behind someone singing and listening to insects shave their legs and then: PAAARRRRRPPPP!

Then I would, indeed, have been volatile, to say the least, as I once became in the Morrisons' carpark in Bridport when I was bent over and adjusting my gaiters (after another walk) while accidentally occupying a disabled parking place. Tooted at, I turned in rage to face a family in another SUV.

'There are a million parking spaces, so why choose this one?' I said in an irate tone.

The tooter, who was the husband, had the decency to remain silent, but his hard-faced wife, quickly out of the car, led the charge, aided and abetted by two fiery daughters in leggings and comely matching bomber jackets: 'She's disabled and we need to get as close as possible.' Granny merely grinned as they installed her in a wheelchair; with such champions she needed to say nothing.

I realised I would never win but added, 'I can see that – but surely a wheelchair admits of some range, some flexibility when it comes to making the heady transition from car to disabled friendly superstore?' Well, not exactly those words, but that was the gist as I huffed off with their tribal jeering in my ears from all but Gran and the hubby, who still kept schtum and who realised that tooting a man when he's down and adjusting his gaiters is tantamount to asking for a fight.

So no toot now.

But instead the eerie silence, like the night sound of a heron's wings flying overhead with the bird invisible in the twilight; the eerie silence of the electric car almost immediately going very fast and very silently past me and my first thought being: for how long has it been dogging me thus? How long had I been like the man with the red flag walking in front of the dreaded motor-beast-car circa 1904? * Perhaps for ten or twenty minutes, I flattered myself, but then realised it was in part due to the surroundings. A walker in the Morrisons' carpark is a mere marginal, a scumsucker on the edge of respectable consumer existence (buying cars and parking them in supermarkets being the main hobbies of the hoi polloi), whereas out here in a national park I had higher status. Indeed, the electric glider who waited so patiently behind me could well have been a walker themselves, albeit one equipped with *too much car*.†

I thought about that mystery driver for quite a while after that.

Then I had left the road and was traipsing across empty

---

* In actual fact, the law was finally repealed on 14 November 1896, when the Locomotives on Highways Act scrapped the necessity of a car requiring a man with a red flag to walk in front of it, and raised the speed limit to 14mph.

† I read today of an Austrian OAP who on retirement gave up his car *en principe* and bought two canoes instead. One inflatable (which he could take on the bus with his free bus pass) and one made of fibreglass that went on a trolley behind his bike, which he could take on the train with his free train pass.

moorland riddled with old mine workings, as much of the land west of Coniston is. It is the land of *Pigeon Post*, of Squashy Hat the mining engineer, where Ransome mixes a real copper mining operation started by his friend Oscar Gnosspelius with his childhood experiences of prospecting for minerals, always with the lure that gold rather than iron pyrites is in the miner's pan. In fact, it was *Pigeon Post* that set me on course for wanting to be a mining engineer, an ambition I had for several youthful years, at least before I discovered that people were more interesting than things. At a crossroads, a couple who I guessed were in their sixties asked me the way as their phone was dead. I was able, with considerable pleasure, to show them on my 1:25,000 scale map, which I told them was my father's and dated from 1983. This did not impress them as much as I had hoped, though the women jauntily added, 'Suppose I need to put that "Oh Christ, I'm fucking lost" T-shirt back on again', and we laughed heartily.

The last words spoken to another human being for thirty-five hours. But I'm getting ahead of myself.

Up and down, and past small tarns and the sign to Torver. No mountain bike tracks for a while, but then I saw some – but not the usual splayed out and rutted spaghetti muddy mess of them, just a couple of thin dry ones, lone explorers. I patted myself on the back for being in a part of the Lakes that was still decently remote. Lunch on a wide rock resembling a giant slice of cake. I lay back on the triangle of it and saw my second golden eagle of the trip riding the thermals with immobile, great-winged ease.

I am enjoying the solitude. This is a wonderfully empty part of the Lakes. If you get away from the, er, lakes, most of it remains pleasantly empty . . . But the question going through my head is: would this make good country in which to go to ground? Build your own survival shelter and underground tunnel complex? The extension of the island hideaway that has been nagging at me for so long?

I mean, am I serious, will the shit ever really hit the fan in my lifetime? People have been predicting the downfall of capitalism and the end of the world as we know it for a very long time. The sensible thing to do would be to remain sceptical. And yet thousands of people are living as if the world will end pretty soon. In America, there are communities where this has been going on for decades . . . where the survivors are dying off, all too aware of the irony of being outlived by the fragile world order.

The fact is, the simple limits of short human life are going to get you far sooner than a global catastrophe of systemic breakdown. But what if . . . I know the interconnectedness of world trade and the just-in-time delivery system and everything being on the internet and all . . . But still, there is an awful lot of empty space in Britain. Let's say there is a total breakdown; then people could cultivate any field they found themselves next to. Cities would starve, of course, but, before that, presumably they would slowly empty . . .?

No, I'm falling into the age-old trap: survivalist thinking is based on a *desire* to see things collapse, an innate destructiveness that finds no outlet or insufficient outlet in everyday life. There is no generalised 'way to survive'; rather, the mechanism – pandemic, revolution, war – is actually the most important factor in predicting the aftermath, which is after all the response. In a way, it's the reverse of the revolutionary who cares only for the imminent destruction of the system.

He has a hundred plans for smashing things up – kidnap, terror bomb, agitprop, murder – yet plans for what happens after the revolution remain hazy.

Ransome was bewitched by the enthusiasm and energy the Russian Revolution released; the whiff of cordite, the smell of revenge excited him too. This was the boy who had been bullied and ridiculed from prep school until he was able to finally master billiards at Rugby, aged fifteen, and develop a certain louche respect. A boy who had left school early, whose writer father had been at Oxford and become a professor who knew everything. With his father dying when Arthur was thirteen, Ransome never had the chance to reject him; instead he chose to idolise and idealise his world of books. And how Arthur loved books: he amassed a library as soon as he could. But this is not the whole Arthur, who is actually an adventurer, a bit of a chancer, a tale teller like his wayward grandfather. When Arthur bought Robert Burton's *Anatomy of Melancholy*, he simply looked at it on his desk for several days. He was thrilled with the fact that he actually owned such a high-status object – him, the kid who kept mice at prep school and was taunted as a fool, a boy who couldn't catch a ball or defend himself.

I know one writer whose 'first book' was Paul Brickhill's *Reach for the Sky*, the story of the war hero Douglas Bader; the writer came from a bookless household and when he read this, aged sixteen, it was the first time he actually enjoyed a book. From then on he was hooked. My own first enjoyable book was *The Island of Adventure* by Enid Blyton (of course it was!). I see this as the plastic kit version of Ransome's reading of *Robinson Crusoe* aged four.

The problem of being a writer who is also an outdoor

type is that he has to do physical damage to himself to get books written. The real egghead is born the shape of an armchair. Ten hours in a library is heaven, not hell, to them. But the writer who is an outdoor type writes with effort. It strains the system. His digestion is shot because without outdoor stimulus he needs tobacco and coffee to get the engine started. Arthur, like Hemingway, is addicted to fishing and sailing and hill walking, because without these pursuits he'd very quickly die from the unhealthy life he was living. Martha Gellhorn said that when she lived with Hemingway he'd spend the morning writing (standing up because of piles and other assorted health issues) before finally curling up in an armchair to read detective stories. Once a week, on Saturday, he'd go out and get rat-arsed with his mates down at the local bar. Then, when this writing schedule finally got to him, he'd allow himself some free time to go out in his boat to catch some marlin. That's when he would recover.

Writers are timid folk or they become timid by writing. The macho types then compensate by doing manly sports, but it's a losing battle. Ransome is always fighting a losing battle. He is always torn between the mythical library beckoning him and the need to honour his childhood 'real self' who wants to fish and sail.

But why his support for the excesses of the Russian Revolution? A conflict in which millions either starved or perished. Though the Russian Civil War, which was the result of the Revolution, saw atrocities on both sides, it was the unconcerned brutality of the Reds that now seems prophetic of the mass killings carried out by Stalin and Mao. (In one significant instance, Lenin asked to see a list of how many prisoners were in the Peter and Paul Fortress in St Petersburg.

Reading the list of 1,500, he put an 'X' at the bottom. A new aide, unschooled in Lenin's ways, misinterpreted the 'X', which simply meant 'I have read this document', to mean 'shoot them all'. Which he did. Lenin was slightly annoyed when this happened but nothing more.) The fact is, despite his social conventionality – and many revolutionaries are socially conservative – Arthur wants to see Rome burn. The destruction of the old and far from perfect Russia is a thrilling prelude to the destruction of the system that humiliated him. Yet Arthur always protests he was never a revolutionary and that it was simply the atmosphere of everyone mucking in and being selfless that drew him to revolutionary Russia. That, and a burning desire to counter the outright *lies* in the right-wing press at the time.

Arthur the truth teller. The boy who was accused of lying about his ability to swim. The boy who becomes John in *Swallows and Amazons* and is incensed when his honour is impugned. I remember reading that as a kid and thinking, well, I'd just accept that Captain Flint was a miserable bastard and that'd be that. But Arthur is projecting an adult reaction onto a childhood humiliation. He had become a truth teller not because of any love of the truth, but simply to 'prove them wrong'. When you're a kid, the adult world simply doesn't make sense except as a way of satisfying your own demands, wants, needs. The adult world is simply insane from a kid's perspective and for many of us, the enlightened ones,* it remains broadly insane, albeit with greater detail and more pitfalls.

Hence my need to escape, find the bolthole; hence

---

* Come on, where's your sense of humour?

Arthur's need to sail and fish and so utterly immerse himself in the world of Swallows and Amazons. But to return to John's reaction to being called a liar. The 'adult' Ransome has raised 'telling the truth' to a pillar of his personal morality. But as one Foreign Office official remarked, 'Mr Ransome is a man chiefly interested in himself and the lady referred to.* He is without conviction or morality. He has always sided with the winning side . . . Ransome always reports the truth as he sees it, the problem is he doesn't see straight.'

Ransome believed in the imperial virtues of Britain, our right to rule the waves. And so it was natural for him to want to interfere, take sides. Yet even here he is timid. He reports the political views of the Bolsheviks without saying what he thinks of them, while all the time being a bit obsequious: 'Not only is [Lenin] a man without personal ambition but, as a Marxist, he believes in the movement of the masses . . . his faith in himself is the belief that he justly estimates the direction of elemental forces.'†

And what he wrote about Lenin is, well, *a bit silly*. 'Lenin struck me as a happy man and walking down from the Kremlin I tried to think of any great leader who had a similar joyous happy temperament. I could think of none. Napoleon, Caesar, did not make a deeper mark on history than this man is making: none records their cheerfulness . . .'

Using GSOH to rank men who bought a place in the history books through inflicting a great deal of death and misery on the world is appealingly childlike but not very sensible.

---

* Trotsky's secretary, who he first romanced and later married.
† *The Truth about Russia* (1918).

Of course, Arthur is really a pirate (Captain Flint, retired 'pirate', in all his lovable silliness and mistakes *is* Ransome), so when the British government ask him to become a spy he accepts straightaway. Ransome had been bullied and mocked and had to scrimp and save and write books about exercise and Oscar Wilde before, finally, yes, being offered a seat at the high table with all his old persecutors. He had made it. Of course he said yes to being a spy.

At the same time, he writes a book exonerating the leaders of the Revolution and saying it really isn't so bad. His own words: 'I am well aware that there is material in this book which will be misused by fools both White and Red. That is not my fault.'* In other words, he refuses to take responsibility for the effect of his words. Foresight, judiciousness – these are not childish qualities, nor Ransome's.

Ransome wants everything, he wants the whole jar of sweets, the whole sweetshop – just like every kid does. Instead of becoming a fully signed-up spy, he becomes an informer for the Brits using his privileged access to the Bolsheviks (he's screwing Trotsky's secretary for Chrissakes).† He loves the energy of the Revolution and he hates the lies being told about it, so he decides to 'tell the truth'. But his 'truth telling' is always at the service of what is really going on: he's in love and he's breaking free of his wife in a culture that thinks that's OK and isn't judging him. He

---

* *The Truth about Russia* (1918).

† Curiously, when I was in Mexico City and visiting Trotsky's house I was surprised to learn the great revolutionary had six secretaries working twenty-four hours a day in three shifts (kind of like being online all the time) and of course it was a man who was shagging one of his secretaries who ice-picked him. Trotsky was obviously addicted to dictating – so much so that he was *secretary blind*.

knows it's wrong but 'telling the truth' is his moral palate cleanser.

Interestingly, in Ransome's comments on Dzerzhinsky, the Bolshevik revolutionary who heads the first secret police of the USSR, forerunner to the NKVD and KGB, Ransome alights on the myth that this Jesuitical torturer took on the lowliest jobs in prison, including mucking out cells, as part of a moral code that elevated doing the dirty jobs that others wouldn't do for the benefit of all. The job of policing the Revolution is just another 'dirty job'. Any familiarity with prison life reveals that dirty jobs aren't so simple: they allow access around the prison and multiple hiding places that squeamish guards avoid. Arthur the storyteller prefers the myth to the uncomfortable and rather obvious reality. A man becomes the chief of a gang of vicious secret policemen because he wants to – if he lacks a conscience. If he has a conscience, he becomes a hypocrite and invents a good reason for taking on and keeping the job. Surely the only really conscientious move is to resign? Only the corrupt imagine they can change things 'from within'. Or the naive. As the old Russian proverb has it, 'Everything that goes into a salt mine becomes salt.'*

History has not only been unkind to Lenin and Trotsky, it has proved them to be the architects of thousands of deaths and untold misery. In the perhaps futile game of speculative history, the picture of Russia continuing to modernise from its feudal beginnings presents a brighter image than the collectivisation famines wrought by Stalin. I suspect a

---

* And in a Stalinist gloss: quite a few things go into a salt mine and *never* come out.

quarter of the misery in the world is caused by people in too much of a hurry. And the other quarter is caused by people opposing those in a hurry (the final half is the misery we bring on ourselves).

In the final, rather brutal analysis, I believe that Ransome, in order to get his leg over, started to see Russia through the eyes of his beloved. When he realised what catastrophic real-world consequences this entailed, he finally retreated into childhood and wrote *Swallows and Amazons*. He also persuaded his Russian second wife, Evgenia, to sign this curious document: 'Dear Arthur, I hereby promise you on my word of honour that I will undertake no political commissions in England from the Bolsheviks or any other political party, and further that I will engage in no conspiratorial work whatsoever without expressly informing you that I consider this promise no longer binding.' Now that is one *strange* pre-nup.

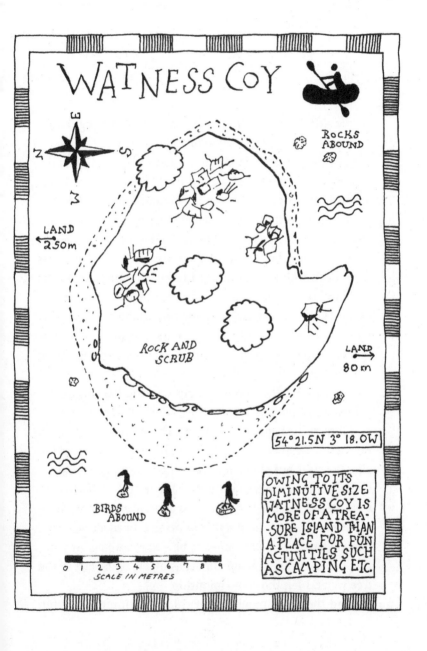

WHITE CUBE

By the side of a deserted C-road, just as I was getting thirsty, I spotted a huge plastic cube of water, bracketed in a steel cage, with a little black tap dripping ever so slightly and a sign enjoining me to partake for free! And a couple of blue Tardis Portaloos too. This was an 'honour' campsite and this spirit of generosity, which touched me deeply, is fairly absent elsewhere in the Lakes, maybe out of ham-fisted necessity, as the groaning burden of a million trips in VW wagons has to be dealt with somehow. But I began to think that maybe this kind of trust is brought out precisely because so many money-grubbers are charging for carparking and camping, etc. I was struck by how we often assume good behaviour will somehow *disappear*, when bad conditions actually bring out the best in people, albeit in the few.

The sign for the honesty camp indicated an Instagram presence: @honestyhutwallenrigg. The fact of this internet au-faitness (Instagram conveying a certain hip quality for a business), together with the pleasingly off-grid nature of the site, the neat but character-revealing (nature appreciative, liberal-minded, craft/maker person) style of the handwritten sign; all this conjured up a perhaps entirely erroneous image of the owner of the honestyhut as being a small, dark, curly-haired woman who I imagined to be always smiling. Anyway, this image cheered me up almost as much as the fact of the free water. I felt the companionship.

And then, not much further along Hummer Lane (en

route to Hummer Bridge and in front of an odoriferous hill called The Hummers – all right, both odour-free but that is their name), I saw the sea! 'Thalassa, Thalassa,' I said far more loudly than I needed to, but there was no one around and I love saying it because of my childhood experience of going on holiday. As we came over the last hill and could *feel* the glow of the sea (you just knew), my dad, who had a classical education unlike his children (I sometimes felt it was like having a father who grew up in Tsarist Russia and, having swapped sides, had risen well within the party but still, alone and at home surrounded by his family, found solace in reminding all of the glories of the past) and remembered his Xenophon, would get us all to say 'Thalassa, Thalassa' in honour of the sea.* I loved this and though my father, unlike Ransome's, did not get me learning Latin aged four or even five, I really would have liked that too, but he was far too modern for that, as I have indicated.

And later, when I read the book *Missee Lee*, in which the Walker children are forced to learn Latin, and are all poor and unenthusiastic students (apart from Roger, who for the first time gets to be the hero), you can't help feeling that Ransome is bringing out his own dunderheaded experiences at school. Yet when I read that, I *knew* I would have been even better than Roger. I was a swot when it came to learning languages. As long as the teaching was strict and involved lots of vocabulary and grammar tests, I prospered: I was the kind of kid who thrived under bitter, arcane and utterly uncreative teaching conditions . . . And just when I

---

* 'The Sea! The Sea!' For those of you without the benefit of a classical education.

arrived in secondary education, those sorts of approaches were being dismantled and replaced by the new maths, by statistics instead of mechanics, and social history instead of the stories of kings and queens. For my whole childhood, I was always looking backwards and imagining the better education afforded to my forebears.

I still know barely a smidgen of Greek, despite a few adult attempts at learning it; I realised that I had now entered a more utilitarian phase of life in which only things I could use (rather than show off about) were what my small and precious stock of motivational juice would be spent on. I would not squander it on well-meaning projects designed to make me more like Arthur Ransome or any other well-educated gent (though Ransome went up the science side of school, so only prep-school Greek for him, too).

But at least I can still enter that privileged and joyous childhood state of pretending I know something only others have mastered by saying, 'Thalassa, Thalassa', as I did now – and marvelled at the great expanse of light released by being near the sea. This is how we know when to say these words: because of that burgeoning brightness I alluded to earlier. Sometimes you are mistaken (a weird atmospheric freak of sun and reflecting cloud can mimic the brightness of hidden sea) and sometimes it is two or three hills in advance of the final one, the view-giver, but once you have experienced this sudden first view of the wide and endless ocean, right there, just waiting, then the light conditions are imprinted: you are wired for sea-sighting.

Hummer Lane, Hummer Bridge and then . . . the Euro-woods! A great plantation of trees to be lost in. Less a track than a trudge, a flat ladder of mud caterpillared into ruts, the sound of chainsaws hanging in the damp air. Through sparse larch and fir a glimpse of hi-vis jackets, red-painted Kubota diggers and draggers, the whole operation exhaling sawdust and sound; the high whine of wood that would prefer not to be cut.

Parts of the Eurowoods (it was managed by some faceless corp and not the Forestry Commission) were taped off and draconian signs indicated random walkers were not welcome. I deviated away from the action to find myself fighting through close-packed spruce with the dry, dead, grey-brown of an airless and needly forest floor, and with the skinny, leafless, spriggy twigs the only growth to be seen, not a bird or a bush about. To get through this sort of manmade forest, you have to plot a route. You can't just follow between two rows of trees, because nature has nevertheless buggered up the order somewhat. Made her presence felt. Some trees have failed, fallen, rotten or died. Others have burst forth, taken more than their fair share of light and land. Roots rise up. The line between trees squeezes and expands; and so you plot your own route; like changing lanes on a motorway, you flip between lines while hoping not to get walled in by too much growth, and aiming for the open spaces you can see ahead.

Following old walls, I find myself in a landscape of tussocky grass surrounded by forest on all sides. There is an old hut reminiscent of a Swedish horror film. All is silent and creepy and not a soul to be seen anywhere. But in front of the hut, on an ancient gate post – a rock with a post hole in it – there is a lizard sunning itself and I have enough time to draw him.

More map scrying and compass righting, and I am scurrying along a wooden walkway that was once put in on purpose to carry one over boggy, flat forest ground, but which is now long forgotten and starting to rot. The walkway reminds me of similar paths in Japan around ornamental lakes, through reeds, with a glimpse of peaty, dark water every now and then under the duckboards. First Sweden, now Japan: the Lake District is living up to its shape-shifting nature; it is truly the place par excellence on which to project an inner landscape, a fantasy experience.

CHANGING GEAR

There is now a small river to wade, but having wetsock socks I feel more than up to the job. Wading rivers is one of the things I like most about any kind of walk I do. It is something you definitely don't do on a casual stroll. Only hard-core walkers wade rivers. And failing to wade a river can have serious consequences: in *Into the Wild*, Jon Krakauer describes how when Chris McCandless failed to wade the river, he eventually starved to death (after being weakened by wild legume poisoning). To be fair, McCandless faced a roaring torrent and he wasn't a strong swimmer, but the very fact that he was cowed and gave up his attempt to cross the river (for which wading is but one tool in the arsenal) meant that he missed the logging wire a mile downstream and other possible crossing places further upstream. For the first rule of river wading is that there is *always* a place to cross – it just might be miles up- or downstream. Your job is to find it.

Crossing rivers is a bit like paddling to an island: a seemingly innocuous wilderness activity freighted with metaphorical meaning. We wade across the Styx, we cross to dry, different clothes in baptism. As a consequence of never entering the same river twice, we emerge different and cleansed: a sort of death and transformation have occurred. The symbolic nature of wading rivers is a big part of their appeal, as is the uncertainty, the need for improvisation and cunning, the fact that there is no path – you must find your own.

This was not a big river but the stepping stones marked on the map were long gone, perhaps reused in the ancient building I had just passed. By having the wetsocks, the main dilemma of river wading had already been solved: do I wade in boots or bare feet? Unless you have rather tougher feet than normal, don't go in barefooted. Riverbeds are sharp and nasty; sometimes there is glass and rusted wire, and even when there isn't, the pointy rocks make normal step-taking a hesitant and unstable business. But if you wear big, heavy boots without socks, they can get wedged in between bigger rocks and can in themselves offer considerable resistance to a strong current. Self-draining jungle boots are the best thing for wading rivers but in their absence a pair of wetsock shoes or socks will do fine. Equipped thus, you are ready to plan your route.

This is where the real essence of adventure lies – working out for yourself the safest route to follow. It is the drug behind the first ascent, the exploration of unknown lands, the descent of rapids. And it is available to everyone who wants to cross a river where there is no bridge!

At first, it's natural to want to cross at the narrowest spot, but cursory examination will show this is always the deepest at some point. But the widest spot can also hide a deep channel next to one bank or the other. Looking and probing with a stick is how you measure these depths and having a good long thick stick to hang on to is your best aid in river crossing. Poles work too, just not as well.

I crossed now with gingerly taken steps; even the deepest part did not go much higher than my knees. But it was still another river, not taken lightly, a pure adventure in the general slog of making my way to Devoke Water.

Suddenly I am back in the present tense again. I am right there. Up the bank and into a field and a man who looks like a farmer is walking towards me. He has a red face and bulky body under a torn Barbour-type coat. I ask him if this is the path. He replies with a vague friendly gesture, 'It's that way, yes.' The sun is shining. The grass had droplets and is bent over like a wet fringe of long hair. I wade on through them. 'It's a good day to be lost,' said the man and I heartily agreed.

But the man had been too vague and I was lost again and back in the past tense as I think about it. I then took a wrong, short cut up a steep bank full of brambles and almost had to turn back they were so dense. Normally, I pride myself on never being defeated by foliage but fear of ticks is now uppermost in many walkers' minds, including my own. Sometimes as a last-ditch resort you have to fling yourself forward over brambles rather in the manner of a soldier flinging himself over a bed of compacted barbed wire in the First World War, but when you suspect a deer has been there before you and shed its load of loathsome ticks you become more circumspect.

The tick (against which I wear a special pair of tick-proof trousers that seem to work) has changed mightily the experience of the wilderness in Britain.* Now, you have to be careful where you lounge, and careful where you squat, and careful where you wander in shorts. Britain, a place with no real nasty beasts, no mosquitoes to speak of, just a few midges which are never too bad when you have the right head net has now got wall to wall ticks. Scotland is even worse. But what can you do? You can't live in fear. Get your tick repellent and spray your gear and get out there, I tell myself.†

Meanwhile, I am now at long last in proper mountain scenery, a track that leads up to a pass with bare hills on both sides and a few patches of bright green grass nibbled and nuzzled down to bowling-green shortness. The sheep come up and gather round my tent, for this is where I am camping, high up but near a stream. In the night, the sheep bump into my tent and I hit the sidewall to scare them off.

I fret away at night with my wavering head torch and plan the next day's route to Devoke and the mythical island of Watness Coy. I say mythical but it is only mythical because: a) Wordsworth mentioned it, and b) it looks very small on the map, and c) I have never even heard of Devoke Water and suspect for some reason it may not exist. It belongs to that category of places which everyone you mention it to says they have never heard of. This experience can lower your self-belief to the point that you give up the mission, or, as in my case, it makes you feel like a real explorer despite

---

* Rovince trousers, though most permethrin-sprayed trousers work pretty well. Pertex trousers without insecticide are also hard for the ticks to cling to.
† According to wilderness experts, if you remove a tick within nine hours of getting it, your chances of getting Lyme disease are very much reduced.

the fact that the place is there for all to see on every 1:25,000 scale OL6 map (old designation).

I know that the day ahead will involve getting lost and misplaced. And it is not due to the map being forty years out of date, though that won't help. No, the reason is that I am out of focus, unwilling to pay that tiny bit of extra attention needed with map and compass to be assured of spot-on navigation. The fact is, with an OS map, a compass, a knowledge of contouring and basic map-reading skills, you should never be lost in the hills. But a part of me wants to skive, take a risk. Sometimes I have my good navigation head on and this works. The gamble pays off. But usually, the moment I stop paying attention out of sheer laziness, I go wrong. And I accept being wrong as a punishment for being lazy and not paying attention. I have developed my own highly inefficient moral ecosystem for moving through the hills.

It is not dissimilar to how I approach many things and it strikes me that the desire to punish has become a desire to punish myself and I deliberately create situations in which I can be punished. These thoughts accompany early morning movements over the hill and down the other side towards the long road to Devoke Water. It's certainly a new thought, a new way to approach things: that a glimpse of failure is not pursued because of fear of success, but out of a desire to be punished for not trying hard enough. Must try harder.

Nevertheless, I still wander a bit off course, but since the road is obvious it doesn't matter. To avoid a long tarmac plod, I cut across very boggy fields. There are no hedges or fences, so in the far distance I can see cars skimming over what looks like the edge of my field but really they are on the road. Which I eventually join again. Past some holiday cottages and a run-down farm with three dogs guarding it, rushing back and forth and barking, and with the wind rising all the time I am at last almost there. Then, over the last hill, I see all at once the lake smudged with white-topped waves and the island too.

WATNESS COY AND THE SILENT MAN

Devoke Water was round like a dew pond set high up in the hilly landscape, yet it was also big as a reservoir. There was a bare boathouse and jetty where you could imagine ice-cold skinny dipping at any time of year, but not a tree anywhere at all except on the island. The light greens and browns of the heather and boggy, rough grasses were all around the lake, and that was enough. In the middle was the island with its tree, which had grown since 1797 or whenever Wordsworth was here. Arthur Ransome never once mentions Devoke Water or its island, though it would in fact make a jolly good island for burying treasure on.

Ransome rightly uses the buried treasure scale as a true judge of islands, once their place on the camping and general liveability scale has been established. Watness Coy was 1/10 for camping and 10/10 for buried treasure. And 2/10 for ease of access as you have to carry your boat a long way from the nearest road to get to it.

I wandered along the poor path, muddy and up and down along the bank. The wind howled now. The reservoir or lake, as I suppose it really was, overlapped its edges: there was no beach and it was brimful with the rain of the high fells. The

clouds black and white and moving too fast, small moods
of rain and light; there was even a flash of sun from time to
time, a hint of a rainbow in the flying spit off the lake in the
wind. My ears were full of the wind as I sat level with the
island on my tick-proof piece of plastic, which I'd carefully
laid out first. I looked at the island, which had grown from
a collection of rocks to a landmass about twenty feet long,
rising up at one end with its single, slightly stunted tree
leaning over in the wind. The tree had the appearance of
a neglected child, but one fighting back and awfully determined.

I looked across and unpacked the tight roll of the yellow
boat. It was certainly too bright for this landscape, too out of
place, like an emergency of some kind. The waves were not
large but they were constant and white-topped and I guessed
the island might be tricky to get to under such conditions,
though in all honesty it was no more than a hundred yards
away, maybe less. Still, I packed away the boat; it was not
worth getting tipped over just to look at such a small and
deprived piece of real estate. I could see it all quite well from
the flat bank. Having come all this way, I was quite proud
of the fact that I was willing to turn back and not risk it.
Having fallen off various rock faces and endured months
in hospital as a result, it had taken me years to cultivate a
sense of caution. I had no wetsuit or drysuit and it was now
spitting with rain and cold, and a slip getting in or out or
getting tipped over would be a solo adventure I didn't need.
Yes, it was a good feeling to turn back having come this far.

But now I had to get going down a long, wide expanse
of a valley that led off the western edge of the Lake District.
The sea wasn't that far away. The path wound through low

bracken and past some ancient cairns. Then it became indistinct and I wandered in the general direction, fretting about
what I would do when I finally, three miles on, finally got to
the main road. Stone walls started to grow out of the empty
hillside as I lost altitude. It's quite interesting, the way the
seemingly unowned and free tops of hills get more and more
parcelled up as you approach sea level and road level. You
can pass through all the stages of man's evolution in half an
afternoon. From the hunter-gatherer to the pastoral nomad
to the settled farmer, and finally the suburban dwelling made
possible in the remote countryside by the VW in the drive.
The lack of social probity is what attracts me to the higher
remoter places; the freedom of places without boundaries
is what I seek. You can have the buzz of being a criminal
without committing a crime.

The fields get smaller, yet they are still not farmed. Many
are full of brambles and bracken and boggy to boot. It's heavy,
heavy going. Further and further off course, I scramble over
a collapsing wall into a steep wood that plunges downwards
to the escape I seek.

The wood is so steep I hang on to trees, left then right,
like someone swinging through partners on a dance floor.
It's a wood of mainly birch and oak, and I slip up on the leaf
litter, landing on my arse and skidding a good way. Back up
and swearing, I shift the rucksack, allowing me to lower my
centre of gravity. It seems to inch higher with age, and you
have to really lower your hips and arch your lower back a
bit to get the centre down low enough to be stable. I still slip
and slide, though now I'm controlling it.

The wood maintains its steep angle to a high stone wall
topped with a line of barbed wire. This is good in some

ways: such careful exclusion means I am getting close to where people live. On the other hand, it's a pain as I can't get over that wall. Left, then right, clambering over downed trees, I search for a hole in the wall. The wood here feels old and neglected. Time is also getting on. Where will I camp tonight?

Clambering up a massive fallen sycamore tree that has knocked down part of the wall, I get higher and higher, slithering on the dark-green lichen-covered branches. When I'm over the wall I drop down, banging the rucksack on branches I haven't really seen; a heavy landing. When you make such an effort to escape, it's demoralising when your new surroundings are also hemmed in. This time with rocky outcrops, bramble patches and close-packed youngish firs.

By now, I was really at my lowest ebb. Walking alone is to experience a series of moods that can lead to their ultimate expression or outcome. There is no one to stop the build-up, or each mood's trajectory. Mood is always habitual; one (me, maybe you too) experiences the same moods in a regular cycle and the mood knows how to build itself. The mood takes over, it likes being boss. Finally, the mood gets to the furthest point it can go. Sometimes that wall is broached by hilarity, an unexpected roar of laughter at the stupidity of it all. Sometimes it is a simple 'fuck it' that undoes the Gordian tangle you find yourself in. Sometimes it is an appeal to something much bigger, external, the gods themselves. The phrase 'trust in the gods' came from nowhere and very quickly, almost immediately, became my mantra. Just repeating it revved me up no end. I was as if reborn. All energies returned and I surged on.

Time to bulldoze through high bracken; there are times

you just have to go for it. And I am rewarded on looking downhill with the sight of a black 'S' of road not so far distant and a white van reflecting evening sun off its windscreen; a flash and it's gone.

I set the compass for the road and decide to go direct. Trust in the gods.

An old deserted farmstead, overrun by sheep, which now functions as a series of degraded sheep pens. There is a 'street' between buildings with metal hurdles blocking off doorways, bound in place with orange binder twine. Straw and sheep muck under foot. For some reason, sheep droppings are much more acceptable than cow pats, which very quickly can turn any level area into a slurry pond.

The fight isn't quite over. A couple of fences to scale and I resolve next time to bring the committed trespasser's tool: a strip of thick canvas, puncture proof, for draping over barbed wire.

Finally, a great relief to hit the thing I have just spent two days avoiding: tarmac. What we seek in the hills is not escape but change. The curse of modern life – if there is one – is the way change isn't built into our lives, we have too much control. Sunday closing is a good example. Once forced on us, we changed our lives on Sunday. But now you can do all your shopping, watch a Netflix movie at 3 a.m. and order in a gourmet takeaway. We are not wired to implement change: for millennia we reacted to change, sought to bring it under control and return ourselves to the steady path. Today, we have to budget in change to our lives; kicking and screaming, my conservative soul must be forced to go on adventures I afterwards consider my greatest achievements.

And now as soon as I start walking I feel my energy begin to wane. The small road I am on feeds eventually into the A-road where I glimpsed the truck so many hours before. It is now about six thirty in the early evening and I have a choice.

Go right to Ravenglass and the sea. Sleep rough on the beach and catch a train and bus combination back to Coniston, where the car is waiting patiently under dripping trees. Or go left and hitch the forty miles back.

Hitching! In the past I've always had luck hitchhiking. Once I got a single lift for a thousand miles while hitching with another guy, his half-husky dog and a great deal of gear. I stick out my thumb and start walking.

I know that it always works better to face the oncoming traffic. And that's when it hits me. I am hitching in a pandemic. Should I wear the mask or not? But hitching in a mask looks like a holdup man on the run. I put on a blue and white paper mask and stick out my thumb, trying to make eye contact with incoming drivers. It usually helps. Except this time I know it is hopeless. Hitching in a pandemic – what was I thinking?

Turn back? My pace falters. My feet develop the extreme achiness I know is a killer for road walking. I am stuffed. Should I camp in one of these fields? But there are houses every so often along the road, nowhere seems hidden enough. The hopeless feelings build, the mood is carrying itself to its conclusion and then . . .

I am gripped all of a sudden by the insane desire to walk those forty miles, or at least continue left and walk until I drop. Even though it is the *wrong* decision, surely. Right means about four miles backtracking on tarmac at most, admittedly uphill at first. No, left it shall be. The new mantra takes hold and I belt out The Proclaimers' line 'And I would walk 500 miles'. The pain in my feet goes immediately. I feel a kind of shrinking in, a compacting, the inner energy of the decision conserving any energy I have and allowing it out only as walking power. It is for moments like these that I get out in the wilderness, I tell myself.

The road itself is straight, not too narrow and with a path some of the way. Mostly, though, I alternate hiking on the verge with facing the oncoming traffic. I am fearless, striding on, full of this bursting-out energy that comes from simply making the right decision. I don't know why, but it is.

And now I am looking for a pub to get some food and a bit of rest; not to stay there since they're all so damn expensive in the Lakes, but just to get enough respite to help me continue my forty-mile road walk. But each village is somewhat gentrified; these are not holiday cottages but the rising house prices that allowed generous loans for home improvements have made their mark. Everywhere looks a bit prosperous.

But then things get more run-down. Another village. A post box in front of a closed post office. I hoped the pavement would continue into the countryside. It did for a while but eventually faded into the verge, becoming thinner and more overgrown until it disappeared under foppish encroaching grass. Now I was on the verge again, careful of the half-hidden feeder dips from roadside to ditch. At regular intervals these break up the level boundary of the verge and make walking slower and more awkward.

My longest previous continuous road walk was not that long: the twenty-eight miles through Birmingham while walking the Great North Line on a hot June day. No, hold on, thirty miles from Baïgorry to Biarritz, in the foothills of the Pyrenees, mostly at night. Nasty blisters resulted, I was tiptoe limping by the end. Mostly, I have been pretty successful at avoiding long stretches of road and here I was contemplating a forty-miler . . . What the hell was I thinking? I was self-contained and full of gumption.

It was getting dark now and cars coming my way were signalling their approach to hills with wayward search beams, floodlights that blinded me as they topped out and locked on for descent. I pulled my beak brim lower and tightened my shoulder straps in much the same frame of mind as the dwarves in *The Hobbit* tightening their belts, except I wasn't that hungry. Well, just a bit.

I was about to walk off the map and then I did. It was

a grand feeling but also made me somewhat nervous that
I might end up near to the sea. Another village came and
went, and up ahead was a white, grimy-looking building by
the roadside that I spied as a former pub now closed. But as
I approached I saw a trestle with a blackboard sign saying
'open'. At last a rest and a plan began to form.

The pub was empty except for two men at the door, one
younger and one older with a moustache, both friendly as I
walked in and became the most interesting thing to have happened on a Sunday night for a while. The barman was a young,
dark-haired and thickset chap, also friendly. I asked for a pint
and two packets of crisps as they had stopped serving food, it
being past 9 p.m. I stayed at the bar with throbbing, humming
legs after all the road walking. I could feel the concrete setting
in my legs. The barman was helpful but hardly communicative.
He told me he was looking to get trade work, building work
in preference to working in the pub.

The older of the two men, though really they were a
double act, told me, 'You'd be better off staying here tonight!'

'No chance of a taxi, then?' I asked and they tittered, but
when I repeated the question to the bartender to make sure
he knew I was serious, he said he might have a mate who
was free.

He dialled his phone and started talking to his pal. I heard
him pause and then say, 'That's what *you* have to tell *me*.'

I warmed to this dark-haired lad, he wasn't setting me
up. He wasn't conniving against me with his mate, trying to
screw the tourist out of all his money for a late-night ride to
Coniston. His mate finally gave a price: 'Thirty-five quid?'
the barman asked me, hand over the mouthpiece. I had been
prepared to say no at £40, so this was a bargain.

I ordered another pint and retired jubilant to a table to wait and make notes on the walk. The two men debated the price of a good sheepdog, which had gone from £50 ten years ago to over £1,000 now. Then one of them spoke in tones that conferred professional awe but personal disquiet of a rapid pig processing plant that killed 11,000 pigs a day – 300 an hour. He had a friend who . . . killed there.

The driver arrived and was waiting outside. As I was leaving, the bartender told me, wistfully I felt, 'We've some beautiful country up there, not so well known as the rest of the Lakes, but beautiful all the same.' I agreed gushingly as part of continued thanks for the rescue, but he wasn't wired for flattery and glad-handing and just nodded me farewell.

It was a long, swervy drive in the dark. Instinctively, I knew that the driver expected no chat, nor did I wish to make chat just for the sake of it, though the darkness outside was oppressively dark and all-enveloping. The journey took about an hour, and he dropped me right at the campsite where the car was parked. I walked with my head torch in the darkness, not even the lake was visible. The click of the car responding to the key fired at distance was ever so reassuring. The damp and cold inside the car did not bother me at all. Round by the boot, I fired up the stove for a hot chocolate and then sat reading in the driver's seat cranked back for a while. To put up a tent seemed an unnecessary fag. There was enough room in the back if I laid the back seats flat and lay diagonally. More than enough. I had two sleeping bags and two inflatable mats. Luxury. I slept well, knowing that the next day I had to be in Wigtown for its book festival.

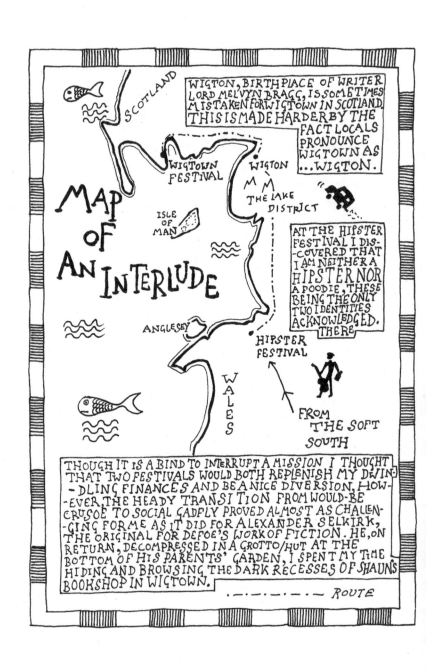

MAP OF AN INTERLUDE

SCOTLAND

WIGTON, BIRTHPLACE OF WRITER LORD MELVYN BRAGG, IS SOMETIMES MISTAKEN FOR WIGTOWN IN SCOTLAND. THIS IS MADE HARDER BY THE FACT LOCALS PRONOUNCE WIGTOWN AS ...WIGTON.

WIGTOWN FESTIVAL

WIGTON

THE LAKE DISTRICT

ISLE OF MAN

AT THE HIPSTER FESTIVAL I DIS--COVERED THAT I AM NEITHER A HIPSTER NOR A FOODIE, THESE BEING THE ONLY TWO IDENTITIES ACKNOWLEDGED THERE

ANGLESEY

HIPSTER FESTIVAL

WALES

FROM THE SOFT SOUTH

THOUGH IT IS A BIND TO INTERRUPT A MISSION I THOUGHT THAT TWO FESTIVALS WOULD BOTH REPLENISH MY DWIN--DLING FINANCES AND BE A NICE DIVERSION. HOW--EVER THE HEADY TRANSITION FROM WOULD-BE CRUSOE TO SOCIAL GADFLY PROVED ALMOST AS CHALLEN--GING FOR ME AS IT DID FOR ALEXANDER SELKIRK, THE ORIGINAL FOR DEFOE'S WORK OF FICTION. HE, ON RETURN, DECOMPRESSED IN A GROTTO/HUT AT THE BOTTOM OF HIS PARENTS' GARDEN, I SPENT MY TIME HIDING AND BROWSING THE DARK RECESSES OF SHAUN'S BOOKSHOP IN WIGTOWN. —·—·—·—·—·— ROUTE

SEVEN

Interlude at a Festival

There were no book festivals in the days of Arthur Ransome. If there had been, he would have been a stalwart of the circuit, I am sure. Kids' authors are always in high demand. And the recently devised Borderlines Book Festival at Carlisle would have been right up his street, not to mention on his doorstep. Arthur Ransome headlining at Cheltenham and Hay-on-Wye! But Wigtown has a very strong children's programme, so maybe he would have found time to go up there and perhaps do some fishing too.

I was up for two festivals this year, Camp Hipster in Wales and Wigtown in Scotland. I've always had more fun and been better treated in Scotland, Ireland and Wales than in England, although that's probably because of the drinking. Camp Hipster had asked me to do a freebie talk in return for nebulous publicity benefits, but had paid me when I whinged, so I doubt if they'll ask me back anytime soon.

Now, I was wandering around in a strange state of mind, still in the Lakes but camping here at the festival. I scored a glamping bell tent and, in a kind of therapeutic 'come down', I scorned the fancy foodie outlets manned by charming public school boys and girls who were having a laugh at the same time. Instead, I used my little gas stove inside the tent to cook up noodles and make tea. I was like a rehoused homeless person who sleeps on the floor rather than in the bed in their new flat.

I helped an artist friend perform his 'act', which involved walking around and dancing with a big plastic head over his real one.* I was just his guide, as he could hardly see with the big head on. A group of people in their thirties – one woman and a gaggle of lads, who were obviously well oiled or high – somehow managed to be both flattering and to take the mickey out of 'Len' (the name of my pal when in character) and then pretended their friend, some yards distant, *really wanted* to see Len dance. We were full of the two-day bonhomie that such festivals trade on, and went over to him. Instead, the lad, nicely bearded, small, well dressed and well pissed, became angry and aggressive at 'the stupidity' of Len's act. There was a punch-up frisson in the air and one of his friends had to chill things out, but the others were just even more amused by the prank they'd played. In the stupid, well-heeled amorality of these goons, I realised that the only festival violence I had ever experienced had been at posh or cool events, never at the cheerful, local, volunteer-run things.

At Wigtown, my favourite festival in the world, I was there to do something much more prosaic: chair events in the first festival since the lockdown of 2020. But while I was there I intended to raid my good friend Shaun Bythell's magnificent bookshop for anything that might help me in my researches into Ransome and the islands in the Lake District.

---

* Steve Chapman aka Stevexoh.

I have never really liked libraries. However, bookshops are different. Academic libraries have been a necessary evil in my life, but mainly I find they put me to sleep. I like public libraries with their plastic-covered tomes and generous lending rules, yet I don't want to hang around in them. When I worked as a courier van driver, my last drop on Friday would be a visit to the Kensington and Chelsea library to pick my weekend selection of books. I always chose off-the-wall titles, things I'd never buy. Often I got lucky: it's how I found out about the autochrome pictures of Leonid Andreyev, the book on posthumous VCs and the exhaustive Henry Wills tome, *Pillboxes*. With the internet you rarely go so far off-field. But a second-hand bookshop, especially a well-stocked one like that of Shaun's, was always a good way to find new and unusual titles.

In the Lake District section, I found a book on looking for Arthur Ransome in the Lake District, an excellent 1970s guide to Lake District ecology, a copy of *The Picts and The Martyrs* (one of Ransome's most underrated books, I feel), a couple of general wildlife guides and two books on Donald Campbell. Quite a haul – but then it is Scotland's biggest second-hand bookshop. I had that feeling of having been egregiously lucky, not quite winning the lottery but definitely a sensation of having stolen a march on life; the feeling you get on eBay when no one else bids for something good that you want. Lucky old me, sitting high up in my bedroom above the shop, making careful notes in my flip-top book of cards.

Every book I write seems to require a different approach to stationary. For one book, I used tiny Europa notebooks and then transcribed the notes at night into an A5 Moleskine. For another book, I switched to a Leuchtturm1917, which I stuck with for a while as I liked the superior page thickness and the natty dot format, not to mention the obscure reference to the turning point year of the First World War for the German forces. But Leuchtturm1917s seem a thousand years away now. For this mission, I was using WHSmith A6 sketchbooks with homemade covers. Super-rugged and waterproof (tested several times) but a bit bulky. They were just a bit oversized and risked falling out of my top pocket into the water when I bent over, so they needed to be waterproof.

At night, I am too tired to transcribe usually, so this A6 notebook must be the record of choice. Some markings on the map, and the flip-top card book for reference facts I discover while reading: lake depths, fish breeds in certain lakes, the size of islands. I thought I'd dislike the flip-top book of cards, held together with a wire spiral, but I really like it. It has the solidity of making notes on card without the bind of losing them or having to keep them in a plastic index card box, which will always open and spill out the cards at least several times during a writing project.

So here I am under the eaves, looking out over the cold chimney pots of Wigtown, a place of very real magic; not for nothing is it a centre of ancient sites, fey people and the first landing place of Christianity in Britain after the Roman departure.

And in a small but real way the magic happens again when I am in the pub on my last night and there are lots of people – writers, locals, hangers-on, festival-goers. I start talking to Ella, a local artist who I have known since I first started coming to Wigtown. We talk about this and that for a while and then I mention Arthur Ransome and the Lakes.

As if ordained by the gods she mentions a good friend in Edinburgh whose mother lives on Coniston and who knew Bridget and Roger Altounyan from the Swallows and Amazons books.

'Wow, that is interesting,' I said.

'What's more, she's visiting me now and is actually sitting over there.'

The friend quickly came over and we started talking. Yes, her mother was aged and slightly forgetful but only about modern events. She remembered very well Bridget and Roger, who had told her in no uncertain terms that Arthur Ransome was a horrible man who didn't like kids. I was a bit taken aback because I still revered the man and it was like hearing someone slander your father or a close relative. But of course later I realised what the two youngest Altounyan children meant. They had been in on the book's creation (well, Roger had, Bridget was too small at first) and then, over the years, had weathered the author's gradual disenchantment with the cheerful clan who had initially inspired him. It was fuelled too by his partisan and highly opinionated wife Evgenia, who knew how to stoke an argument and provoke a dispute. And Arthur, being a bit silly and easily led, like many authors, followed. And somewhere down the line he lost his sense of humour.

Often it goes when one's energy goes. Arthur simply lost his bounce. He'd always joked that kids were brats and called them that. But one day the wind changed and *those* kids *were* brats and it wasn't funny anymore. It's what happens when you don't pay attention to the fork, the fork in the road that is coming your way all too fast and all too soon. If you don't decide what kind of person you are, or how you'll be when you don't have energy and strength anymore, then lack of energy and strength will define you, stamp all over your life, make you irritable and old maid-ish, narrow rather than open, inward-looking – rather than spreading your hands up to the sky and thanking the world for it all.

But I still didn't know all that at the time, so I stood slightly stunned at this hatred, or at least strong disapproval of my hero, and didn't know what to say. I mentioned Donald Campbell instead.

'Oh,' said the friend, 'you should speak to my mother; she remembers the day he died. She was watching from the house when he roared by and saw him go up, everything.' Another connection to my past. 'It was the sound she remembered. The noise of him hitting the water. The boat I mean.'

ARTHUR'S DIARY, WINTER 1910

Found while researching:

> 12 November Evening spoilt by Ivy's* Mother. Night ditto; by the sheer ugliness of remembering her.
> 13 November Blues.
> 14 November Blues.
> 18 November Belly bad.
> 19 November Belly.
> 20 November Ill belly.
> 1 December All ill.

---

* His first wife.

A Trip to Paris for Christmas didn't help much.

25 December Blues.
26 December Blues.
27 December Blues. Improvement.
28 December Jolly day. Row about my rudeness when at
dinner with the Gordons.

As I wrote and researched I began to develop stomach symp-
toms alarmingly similar to those Ransome had. I was about
to head back to the Lakes and for some reason I got an urge
to pack ham and mustard sandwiches for the journey. Ham
and mustard was the taste I associated with travel: when I
was a boy, my mum made ham sandwiches for when we took
the ferry to France. We would often eat them at 10 a.m. in
the carpark while waiting in the long queue to board the
Townsend-Thoreson boat.

By the time I reached Penrith, in order to buy yet more
camping supplies (gas bottles almost completely sold out
owing to Brexit/pandemic), I was suffering from real
stomach pain, which I took to be a combination of fearful
anticipation of having to kip in my car (my new plan) and
something to do with all the rum and French *saucisson* I had
been consuming, along with the mustard and ham. Making a
mental note to get it checked out, I proceeded to stage two of
the latest plan, which was to find a carpark near to Derwent
Water where I could continue my researches into islands.

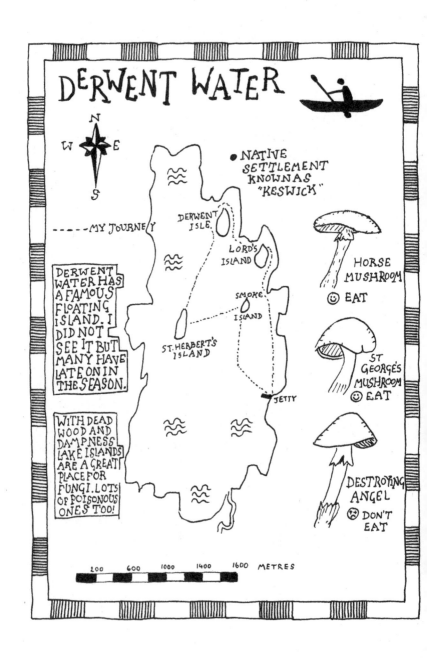

DERWENT WATER

N W E S

NATIVE SETTLEMENT KNOWN AS "KESWICK"

- - - - MY JOURNEY

DERWENT ISLE.

LORD'S ISLAND

SMOKE ISLAND

ST. HERBERT'S ISLAND

JETTY

DERWENT WATER HAS A FAMOUS FLOATING ISLAND. I DID NOT SEE IT BUT MANY HAVE LATE ON IN THE SEASON.

WITH DEAD WOOD AND DAMPNESS LAKE ISLANDS ARE A GREAT PLACE FOR FUNGI. LOTS OF POISONOUS ONES TOO!

HORSE MUSHROOM
☺ EAT

ST GEORGE'S MUSHROOM
☺ EAT

DESTROYING ANGEL
☹ DON'T EAT

200   600   1000   1400   1600   METRES

EIGHT

The Beckoning

Lake: Derwent Water, 22 metres deep, 4.6 kilometres long, 5.35 square kilometres
Islands: Lord's Island, St Herbert's Island, Smoke Island, Derwent Island

Feeling a bit timid and in a certain amount of pain, I found a carpark with no signage prohibiting an overnight stay. It was only a short walk from the lake's edge. I laid out my camping mat and sleeping bag in the extended back of the car and attempted sleep. Every now and then, cars went past on the road. None entered the carpark and a ridiculous fear of being told to move on or worse 'told off' interfered with my multiple attempts to achieve a deep and satisfying sleep. I took another slug of rum, which I knew already to be injurious to my stomach lining along with all the coffee I habitually drink from dawn till dusk. Well, both these bad habits would have to go. Around 5 a.m. I fell into an unconscious state that lasted until about 7.30 a.m.

Then I was up and into my chest waders, stomach almost forgotten, the game afoot. Waders were a new addition to my arsenal of island-exploring kit. The reasoning being that waders (with a belt around the middle) would be a safe form of drysuit if I fell in while paddling in rough water on a cold lake. I had already by now thoroughly absorbed the tale of poor Ted Scott dying after his capsize on Windermere and I had no urge to follow him, as some of the lakes I would be visiting were deep and cold and I was, like an inmate of Alcatraz, fairly softened by a diet of hot showers and baths and very little of what might be called cold water swimming.

So, chest waders. I hadn't used them since 2004 when my team had successfully paddled the Bad River in Canada, and waders had made it possible to walk and swim the boats through glacial water rapids. They were like old friends when I put them on with stocking feet so I could wear slip-on beach shoes to traverse the short distance to the water.

This time, no messing. The wind was up, Derwent Water was rough as hell, waves crashing on the beach. The rain came in misty gusts that emanated from the foggy centre of the lake. Not one island was visible. But the sheer nastiness of the conditions cheered me. This was real at last. Spit-in-my eye nature, wet my hair, blow me down and tear up the lake with waves and foam and birds precariously out on the wing, alert to being blown about. I would certainly be using the inflatable canoe and not the flimsy packraft today. Oh, you'll read about packrafts being used on grade five rapids (the most extreme) but that's on rivers going full tilt. On a lake, against the wind, the Noddy-car bulbousness of the packraft is a serious disadvantage.

I set off in the direction of the first island, as indicated on the map. Its name was Rampsholme, but I'd been to the one on Windermere with the same name so I decided to rename it as soon as I saw it. Paddling on with this thought,

I soon forget my ailments and worries. This was fun! I was battling the wind and rain and slowly but surely making my way towards an unknown island.

The island's trees came down to the water's edge, their roots exposed like a delicate mangrove swamp, albeit a model village mangrove swamp. Should its name be 'Mangrove Island'? No, I saw smoke rising. Smoke Island it was. However, smoke meant people . . . I had to watch the waves. But very close in, the island's shoreline was shaded from the wind. I was able to sneak between large rocks and hop out in my waders without fear of the depth – which was only about up to my knees anyway, but if I had been in trousers that would have meant having damp, cold legs for the rest of the day. But not now!

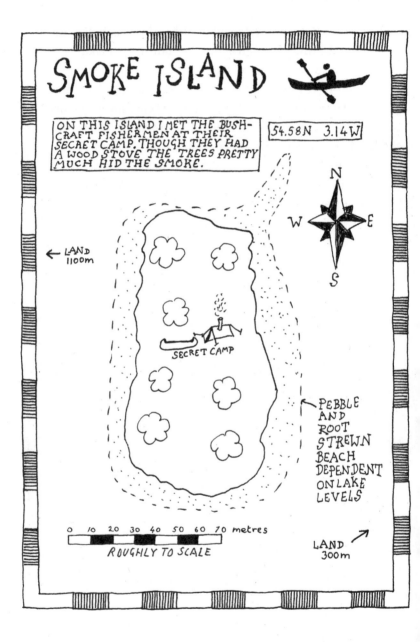

SMOKE ISLAND

ON THIS ISLAND I MET THE BUSH-CRAFT FISHERMEN AT THEIR SECRET CAMP. THOUGH THEY HAD A WOOD STOVE THE TREES PRETTY MUCH HID THE SMOKE.

54.58N 3.14W

← LAND 1100m

SECRET CAMP

→ PEBBLE AND ROOT STREWN BEACH DEPENDENT ON LAKE LEVELS

0 10 20 30 40 50 60 70 metres

ROUGHLY TO SCALE

LAND 300m

Going up the slight slope into the heart of this quite large island (but not so large I couldn't see the full extent of it), I saw at once a covert camp of olive-green bell tent, camo kitchen tarp and green Explorer-type canoe with a silent electric motor. The bell tent had its smoking chimney poking out of a fireproof hole in the roof and I could hear low voices in the tent. Because all this gear meant these were hard-core outdoors folk and not just drunken holidaymakers, I was keen to make contact, and after doing a tour of the island I kept watch on the tent as I suspected they were hiding from me in the way I would have hidden from me if I'd made such a gorgeous camp on just such an island.

The lads came out eventually and were somewhat reserved at first as we all knew that we weren't supposed to be camping. I complimented their tent and titanium wood-burning stove so they got the picture quite quickly.

'Are you fishing?' they asked.

'No,' I said. I asked if they were.

'Yes.' Though they hadn't caught any fish and now, with the rising weather, they wanted to get home. They had all the gear and more: part of the internet generation, raised on excellent how-to videos on primitive technology on YouTube, when the apocalypse comes these lads will be well ahead; though I was a little concerned when I praised their silent electric motor and one gave himself away by saying, 'I like paddling, but I like to have a back-up too.' Said as if a motor was a normal thing, the usual thing and paddling, like analogue photography, was just something you did on sunny days. Motors were like digital, the real thing. But it was a small quibble: here were bearded men (of course) in their twenties with a fish camp that wouldn't have been out of place in . . . Arthur Ransome's time. They even had an axe waiting in a block of wood.

They had camped on all the islands (except the one with a house on) on Derwent Water. They told me Thirlmere had some good islands too, but one was very popular with campers. The more studious of the two, who copied my locution, (I said I'd give something a 'wide berth' and a few minutes later he recommended giving a certain island a wide berth, which was flattering, I must say) told me that St Herbert's Island was the most popular on Derwent Water and always had campers. One time he'd been camping there, 'And it was about 11 p.m. and I heard this noise in the bushes – a kind of crashing sound – and I thought, "That can't be an animal, surely?" So I went out to look and couldn't see anything but when I turned this bloke was right in my face, no head torch, nothing. I was so shocked. "What the hell are you doing?" I said, but he was off his face on mushrooms and thought he was some kind of woodland creature or something. He apologised, though. Before he slithered off.'

The other said he'd been told on good authority by a park ranger that you could buy rolls of fake parking tickets on eBay which matched exactly the ones used in the carpark machines. 'Only a tenner,' they said. But then he conceded that he was a National Trust member so he didn't need to stoop to such low tactics.

I enjoyed meeting these lads and would have stayed longer to chew the fat, but it began raining again and I knew I had to be off to St Herbert's Island, if only because one of my friend Mark's sons is called Herbert. We parted with a quick and friendly dialogue on the use and abuse of phones when travelling. Useful for weather updates but what else?

Ah, phones and the wilderness. Ransome had none of these dilemmas. When he lived at Ludderburn, not so far from Windermere's eastern bank, he would communicate with a fishing pal who lived half a mile away by using triangular, square and diamond-shaped pieces of wood held up against a white wall (the signals were black). His neighbour used white signals against the dark granite-coloured house he lived in. The signals were only used for fishing. And were used to communicate such things as: ARE YOU GOING FISHING? WHICH RIVER? And even: HAVE YOU ANY WORMS? Readers of Ransome's *Winter Holiday* will recognise the signals used there, which had their origin in this fishing-driven communication system.

When I was a child, the idea of walkie-talkies seemed amazingly exciting to me. It remained so and even inspired some of my friends to become CB radio fans. The use of two tin cans joined by string was a tolerated substitute for real walkie-talkies, which never really worked even when you had them. And now the mobile phone makes all communication easy. Except when you can't get a signal. Which is pretty much everywhere in the Lakes. Ransome would have liked that.

Again despite wind and lashing waves, I made it pretty easily to St Herbert's, which was quite a bit bigger than Smoke Island. I landed with care just in front of an arc of sand, a micro-spit of land that went quite a way out. Ashore, I took care to tie up the boat and get it out of the water. All my gear was in the canoe, but tied in, in case of capsize.

For some reason I took my waist pack with me, although I usually stashed it in my roll-top Ortlieb bag.

Tying up my small craft, I was mimicking Squirrel Nutkin and pals when they arrived at Owl Island on their flimsy homemade rafts in the Beatrix Potter story of the same name. St Herbert's, with its many beech and hazel trees, was the model for Owl Island where a large tawny owl called Old Brown required mollifying in order that the young squirrels could go about their nut collecting. However, Squirrel Nutkin annoys Old Brown with his constant silly riddles and chatter – and barely escapes with his life.

I read the story or, more likely, had it read to me in the space between learning to read and getting addicted to reading, an event I can quite clearly date to my reading Blyton's *Off on a Holiday Adventure* aged seven. Already the notion of holiday and adventure were getting welded together in my young and receptive mind. I read the book straight through while I was ill, and then immediately read it again to try to recapture the experience, the sheer excitement of it, which was different to films such as *Chitty Chitty Bang Bang*, which I also loved dearly. The book experience was like a private fantasy, whereas the film experience was more public.

The book was more singular too, less generally acceptable or mainstream. I think I still seek this, perhaps unconsciously, in a book – what others will reject or find eccentric or simply cranky – but the game is not an easy one. I do have *standards*. The book can't simply be a self-published work of esoteric conspiracy; that is not interesting at all. Rather, the book must be accepted in some far distant realm (possibly an imagined Paris or New York of a previous era) and then be found by me. Or discovered on a dusty holiday home bookshelf of a house I am renting or borrowing. It is connected to the idea of treasure, I am sure.

Beatrix Potter's island, then. The author left over 4,000 acres to the National Trust when she died, all in the Lake District. After she married and became interested in acquiring lands and farming them, she wrote far less. Like it was for Shakespeare, real life seemed more interesting to her.

This island was much nearer land than the other one and as soon as I hit the first beech-tree clearing I met a family of four more squirrels in wetsuits.

'Did you swim here?' I asked the youngest, a girl of about ten.

'No, only paddleboard,' as if this was a second-best way to travel.

I nodded at her trendy parents and moved along to find a big camp where young lads in their late teens and early twenties were sort of milling about. Outward Bound or Scouts, I thought, as they all had identical lifejackets.

St Herbert's is actually named after the saint who brought Christianity to the Lakes and who built a cell on the island in AD 685. I rootled around, looking for his cell; there is a kind of overgrown half hovel, half-dugout hole but whether that is the cell that pilgrims even to this day travel to revere, I cannot say.

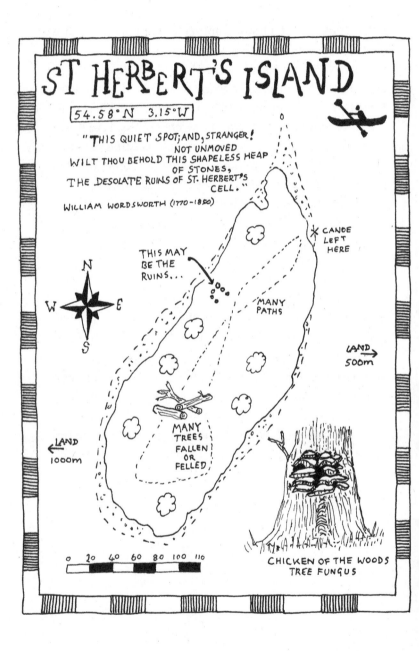

ST HERBERT'S ISLAND

54.58°N 3.15°W

"THIS QUIET SPOT; AND, STRANGER!
NOT UNMOVED
WILT THOU BEHOLD THIS SHAPELESS HEAP
OF STONES,
THE DESOLATE RUINS OF ST. HERBERT'S
CELL."

WILLIAM WORDSWORTH (1770-1850)

CANOE
LEFT
HERE

THIS MAY
BE THE
RUINS...

MANY
PATHS

N
W   E
S

LAND →
500m

← LAND
1000m

MANY
TREES
FALLEN
OR
FELLED

0   20   40   60   80   100   110

CHICKEN OF THE WOODS
TREE FUNGUS

The beech trees, the source of Nutkin's beech nuts, dwelled in the middle of the island. Beech is considered by some to not be a native of these isles, arriving later with Neolithic tribes around 2000 BC. It has a wood easily carved whose name comes from the Anglo-Saxon word *beoce*, related to the German *Buche*, Dutch *beuk* and Norse *bog* and *bok*. Our English word 'book' is derived from the 'rune books' of the Norsemen, which were carved on flat pieces of beech.

I circled back after inspecting various giant felled trees to see a group of lads near my canoe. One was a smiling blond lad with, it seemed, a slight European accent, though I couldn't say what country. He wanted to talk yet it was phoney friendly chat – yes, a nice place this, and what a good time they were having – and that smile was unnecessary; after all, he was a teenager, wasn't he? As I checked my canoe I could see the Ortlieb bag had been opened and not rerolled in the way I do it. Nothing gone (it only contained a pump and a mending kit) but I was annoyed – more at being suckered by the kid than experiencing an incident of petty crime on an island paradise. Young offenders then, I thought, so typical Outward Bound fodder. When I saw some of the lads taking selfies while standing on the end of the spit, which was underwater so it looked like they were floating, I could see they were just having fun, but still I was resentful and paddled off in a huff that lasted only a few hundred metres.

The next island, Derwent Island, was the one with the beautiful house and garden – and lots of 'no landing' signs.

It was an interesting example of the tragedy of the commons. The open-access islands had very little grass, looked tangled and a bit messy, and were often picked clean of useful firewood. But this island looked great, with a curving kempt lawn that came down to the water's edge. The building had an Italianate aspect that was most pleasing. It fell into that category of houses: 'Well, I certainly wouldn't mind living there!' I circled the place low in the water, rain spitting, and with contrary winds at lake level causing confused wave patterns so I needed to keep my wits about me. Freak waves occur when a couple of large waves find themselves in step and double in size and hit from an unexpected angle. But the Tango 200 was as stable as a Scotch pancake on a bedspread so I didn't feel so very unsafe. I could only remember being tipped in a couple of times before: both in wild sea surf when bringing the Tango into shore.

This island had previously been called Vicar's Island and then Pocklington's, after the eighteenth-century eccentric Joseph Pocklington, who built the current house with a fort attached to fight mock battles during lake regattas. He also built a druid's circle, which was quite the thing to have then. Before that, it had been the residence of German miners in the sixteenth century, who had been brought to work here by Queen Elizabeth I. * These early experts had found or worked deposits of silver, lead, graphite and copper.

Wordsworth wrote of Pocklington, creator of the current (and I think rather beautiful) house: 'a native of Nottinghamshire, who played strange pranks by his buildings and

---

* The first time I read this as referring to German *minors*, which conjured up images of medieval hippies.

plantations upon Vicar's Island, in Derwentwater, which his admiration, such as it was, of the country, and probably a wish to be a leader in a new fashion, had tempted him to purchase.' Basically, Wordsworth was like me: against anything new.

On the subject of the house, he continued: 'at the bidding of an alien improver, the Hind's Cottage [. . .] with its embowering sycamores and cattle-shed, disappeared from the corner where they stood; and right in the middle, and upon the precise point of the island's highest elevation, rose a tall square habitation, with four sides exposed, like an astronomer's observatory, or a warren-house reared upon an eminence for the detection of depredators, or like the temple of Aeolus, where all the winds pay him obeisance . . .'

I came round to the front of the island, which had an extravagant boathouse and where a variety of powerboats were moored. More 'no landing' signs. Probably people *did* land when there were no signs, but the power of signage is hard to tell. I once had a parking place outside my house in a sort of lay-by, which wasn't actually part of the road – but people thought it was, so it got parked in until I put up a sign. Even then, it still got parked in, but by a different kind of person – usually tradesmen visiting other houses, who were never there for long. They thought the sign didn't apply to them. In another house, the garage entrance could be blocked. It had an old and worn sign stating this, but vehicles still parked there, including one motorbike, which I am ashamed to say I 'keyed' on its shiny tank out of sheer frustration – yes, you with the midnight-blue Triumph 1200, it was that furtive bearded bloke all the time! So though I naturally loathe all signs, I can see the point of them. Here, one of the signs was actually half submerged as it was nailed to the underside of the dock. Maybe to warn off scuba divers making a deep-sea approach.

My final destination was Lord's Island. It was a haul away back into the eye of the hurricane. Well, maybe force 6. The funny thing about the Beaufort wind force scale is it's so understated: force 6 is just a 'strong breeze'. The rubbery nose of the canoe, already a bit soft on one side (the darned leak had still not been fixed properly) was getting picked up by the gusts of wind and driven inexorably towards rocks near the shore. A single post with barbed wire stood out of the water as an obvious danger point. This being the Lake District, a group of well-meaning grockles stood on the low crags above this windy point, anxious to observe a sea disaster. It was time to pull out all the stops and go into overdrive. Not quite panic overdrive but hard, driving paddling for all you're worth and to hell with how funny you look. Quite a few disasters, I am sure, are caused by an unwillingness to look silly. Well, not me.

With an inch-by-inch clawing against the wind, I rounded the point and then it was fairly easy going to the Lord's Island landing place, which was shrouded by overhanging trees, so much so there was no obvious beach until I got close and saw one hidden under some branches. The island was not that far from land. In fact, in the fifteenth century there had been a drawbridge to the land. What a sensible idea. It was the ancient home of the earls of Derwentwater, but they had all left their island fastness for the mainland by 1623. For a while, then, they must have been neighbours with the German miners, who were known to brew beer and keep livestock on their island. Maybe the earls and the Germans had convivial parties, rowing back dead drunk to their respective islands . . .

I landed, and made my usual exploratory mission around the island, notebook and camera at the ready. It was a bit like a school biology project. One in which a tyrannical teacher forced students out no matter how wet or windy it was. My notebook and pen combo again displayed their admirable ability to work without going soggy and bleeding, and I made sketches and notes that I hoped I would be able to interpret later. Or perhaps it was a history project, as I was now able to see the outline of an ancient building, the last sorry remnant of the earls of Derwentwater. With my 'report writing', it was hard to get away from the fact that I was still doing things in my late fifties that I'd done at school: going to places, looking at things, writing it up for praise or status. My word count was the same as that of the weekly essay I wrote at university (albeit now I did it every day, so . . . some improvement). While others moved on, I remained in school mode, which I connected to my feeling that the best was yet to come . . . There is a kind of optimism in remaining behind. Lots of people do jobs that are nothing like school: plumbers, cowboys, car jockeys and bellhops. But all middle-class high(ish) status jobs are pretty much like school. Lots of writing and waiting and having to pay attention to things that don't really deserve it.* Even a professional golfer is like some ace sports student, the pet of the class. Though I disliked my schooldays intensely, I now live a life that resembles being some sort of

---

* But perhaps to be replaced by AI, with the middle classes facing the same sort of job destruction as weavers in the eighteenth century . . .

student with endless projects to do. My father, who didn't go to school until he was thirteen, later became a schoolteacher . . . Oh well, another conundrum to ponder while I brew up down by the water.

Despite the wind, I get the stove well protected behind the aluminium baking tray I've bent into a windbreak. The hot tea, laced with milk powder and some Canderel sweeteners I got from the McDonald's in Penrith, is delicious.* Looking out across the storm-tossed waters, I see something properly interesting: two Canadian-type canoes lashed together with poles to form a sort of loose catamaran, quite wide, with four people togged up in hoods, rain gear and rain-spotted spectacles who are paddling like mad; well, paddling like people who are rather overwhelmed and not that used to paddling but who are trying hard all the same. It was a fascinating scene because (like the sightseers on the crag had done earlier) I was half hoping for a sea disaster. But the lumbering craft came closer and closer.

A woman with a big, red face and long, blonde hair was encouraging the others and paddling with more gusto. I thought the other three might be recently retired, as they had that tentative look of people who are not used to using their bodies a lot and who are used to keeping in the warm, but who are not yet old – not that I could see them very well. But it was like an interesting test of observation – and writers are supposed to do these things to stay trim – so I looked carefully and thought they were two couples in late middle age. The red-faced, cheery woman was maybe younger, but it was hard to say for sure.

---

* Top tip: loot McDonald's for sweeteners and salt sachets before any camping trip.

I watched the wibbly catamaran as it approached, and I really thought it might break up, as each boat was almost independent of the other when it came to power strokes but hopelessly entangled when it came to wave affronts from the turbulent lake. One hull would be up and the paddlers leaning into air, while the other was deep in a trough. It was a bit like watching a crippled daddy longlegs go ice skating. I thought about my own solution. For a start, one of the mantras of catamaran building is that the whole structure should be supported by a single hull. Everything connected to that – the *amas* (connecting poles) and the other hull – should be quite contentedly supported even when only one hull is actually resting on something solid. This is so the power is transmitted through the hull and not into pushing the hull apart. Secondly, these hulls were far apart. To get a catamaran effect (i.e. massively increased stability), the hulls should actually be quite close together. Especially when paddling rather than sailing, which involves a lot of heeling over in the wind.

Still, by hook or by crook, the imminent disaster I awaited was averted and the ungainly contraption made it into shore, and landed about fifty yards from where I was sipping tea in a contemplative fashion, not being too keen on braving the waves yet again for the return journey. The four, I saw now, were all women and the younger, blonde-haired and red-faced one was their leader. I nodded in their direction but made no further gestures of friendship. As far as I was concerned, they were inept interlopers in my dream of island escape. I could feel the red-faced woman looking over towards me and I dare say I could have hailed her and said 'fare thee well', but the lonely islander in me kept schtum and stirred his tea with a handy twiglet broken from a waterside willow. The catamaranistas were heading into the interior of the island, so while they were gone I paid a visit to the catamaran and saw that ropes secured the connecting *amas* by going under each hull. Putting a rope there would cause a fair bit of drag, I thought, and my opinion of the craft was further diminished – especially in comparison with my own slick craft, albeit a little deflated on the starboard side.

The party of adventurers returned and their leader came over and enjoined me to parley with her as the joint heads of our respective operations, albeit mine being a team of one.

'Fisherman?' she asked.

'No, just paddling,' I said.

'Inflatable?'

'Yep.' I wanted the conversation to persist and felt that, what with her being the outgoing, rugged type that she no doubt was, I ought to say what was on my mind, which burst forth as: 'So . . . what's with the catamaran?'

She took it as a criticism, which it might have been, but like Schrödinger's cat, only if you took the lid off and made sure. But she knew a dead cat when she saw one.

'Why a catamaran? Simples, you don't fall in. End of.' She gestured at the foaming waves. 'Novices can't cope with that!' Pause. 'We're on a historical tour.'

I felt something had been missed out, but I got the picture. She went on, earnest and a bit stern: 'We paddle out and rig a catamaran to sail back. Everyone has fun. No one drowns. End of.'

'Right-oh,' I simpered.

She glared at my supercilious, tea-drinking face. 'This is my job. This is where I work.'

'Jolly good,' I said.

And I thought about a summer I'd spent as an assistant outdoor instructor at Kilvrough Manor on the Gower Peninsula when I was seventeen and a girl there, who was eighteen, asked me if I had in mind a career in this field, which I did not, but she did. I thought maybe I had just met her again, as you do. Except Red Face was about fifteen years younger than me, so it obviously was not the case. But I wanted it to be, so I thought maybe that girl had been trapped in a time warp of some kind, thus slowing down her aging until we met again under these damp and storm-tossed circumstances. It was admittedly not a likely explanation but I liked its ingenuity.

But imagining I was meeting people I already knew had to give way at last to beating back against the tide and the wind to the jetty I had left what seemed like a thousand centuries ago but was in reality only that morning. And it wasn't even teatime yet.

I planned to head to the nearest shore and deflate the canoe on the beach. I was already savouring in my mind the harsh roar of spent air as it gave up the ghost and puddled into a damp roll of puckered canvas, and then walking back from there (I'd drive along the lakeside and pick up the canoe later), but a strange desire to 'do the work' overcame me – and I found a second wind to counter the real wind's second wind and did battle along the shoreline, heading ever southward against the prevailing gusts. Several months of canoeing along wide and inhospitable rivers had taught me how sneaking close to a bank can make life a lot easier. Big, heavy boats fear the shoreline because of the possibility of an awkward shipwreck on submerged rocks or being blown beam end on, onto a lee shore. But a canoe is different. You can be blown onto rocks and bounce off. Or jump out. The perilous shore becomes your friend and, very close to, the wind is in shadow from the trees and inlets, and you can actually make quite good progress.

Slowly and pitifully (probably, when viewed from the bank) but triumphantly and majestically (as majestic as a partially deflated airbag can be) I edged round the lake to the concrete jetty. Waves smashed against it, making getting out difficult. In the end, I landed on the beach where I had set off that morning. It was raining again as I lumbered through the multiple tasks associated with deflation and transport. Back at the carpark, I bunged the whole wet mess in the front-seat area. Luckily, my aging Honda had convenient holes in the floor that let the lake water drain out. All my other wet clothes I draped around the interior, before switching on the engine and the heater, full blast. Before the heater kicked in, I endured the cold, damp air whistling up from the cluttered dashboard. Luckily, after a quick carpark change between two open doors, I was now wearing my nylon romper suit: the Buffalo pile fibre and Pertex dungarees as worn at the Antarctic before better clothes were found. Nineteen-eighties Antarctica was my kind of period – pre-designer, hard core, with a zip that stretched from the small of your back right under the flyover and up to your navel. You never get cold in these things . . . ever.

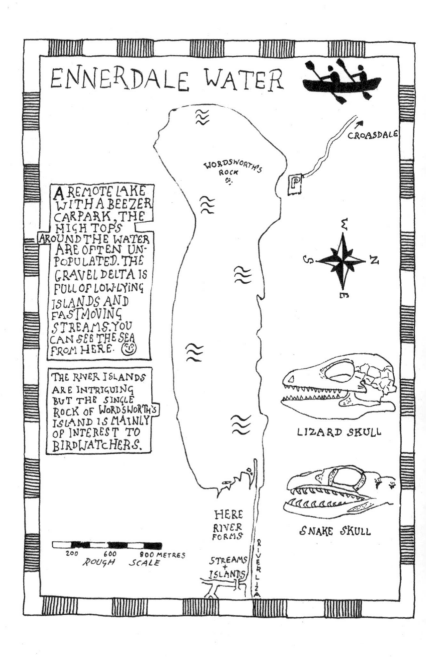

NINE

Mark and Liz

Lakes: Ennerdale, 45 metres deep, 3.9 kilometres long, 3 square kilometres; Loweswater, 16 metres deep, 1.8 kilometres long, 0.64 square kilometres; Crummock Water, 43.9 metres deep, 4 kilometres long, 2.52 square kilometres
Islands: Norway Island, Invisible Island, Woodhouse 1, Woodhouse 2, Gaffer Tape Island

Time for a change. Ennerdale. My good friend Mark the forester had told me there were islands on Ennerdale; at least there were the last time he had been there about ten years earlier. He could meet me there the next day. I left Derwent Water in the early evening and made the long roundabout drive to Ennerdale, right on the western edge of the Lakes. Wordsworth wrote there was a single rock island, where 'the haunt of cormorants and sea-mews clang.'

It was dark when I arrived, driving down the seemingly endless single-track road that ends at the lake. Mark had told me we should meet at the carpark, which was good, because the carpark was king-sized, free and unscrutinised by cameras and other surveillance gadgets (what would these be? DNA samplers working off expelled air?). My headlights on full beam swept the area, which had only two other residents – darkened cars whose owners must have been on a multiday hike and who had left their vehicles there.

Because I was far from other cars and houses and surrounded by pine trees I felt much more relaxed about car camping, i.e. dossing down in the back of the damp and now damply odoriferous Honda. But I was beginning to like my little routines, the brewing up at the back of the wagon with the door up to act as a rain shelter; the slight naughtiness of running a roaring gas stove in the boot with flammable material quite close to hand if it fell over – yes, the danger of being a dangerous camper, oh yes – and then back into my cosy bunk hole lined with multiple sleeping bags and inflatable mattresses, and even an airline pillow cossetting my neck like a flesh-eating clam. A single car left at 9 p.m. Another arrived at 3 a.m. It was like being on a stakeout in a Le Carré novel but one which made no sense and smelt of socks. Wet socks.

Morning. At last. I wondered how on time Mark would be. And Liz. He was coming with his wife, who obviously thought we were having fun doing what we were doing. She'd learn. I was looking at my watch at exactly 8.30 a.m., which was our agreed time, when a car (a brand-new red Fiat 500) pulled into the carpark and hove into a bay some distance from mine. This was not the Toyota estate Mark usually drove; they had come in Liz's car.

Full of the joys of a lonely man at last meeting people he knows, I tripped over to the Fiat in my sky-blue British Antarctic Survey dungarees while still brushing my teeth. I thought this would show how informal I was, how au fait with carpark living. Mark and Liz were staying put in the car, though it had actually stopped raining. It had those trendy darkened windows which I thought showed how 'street' and stylish Liz was, compared to Mark's more utilitarian approach. I bet he hates this car, I thought jovially as I rapped on the back window and gurned towards it with the foaming toothbrush still in my mouth.

Nothing. Pretty rude or playing it cool?

Well, I wasn't taking the toothbrush out just for them. I went round to the driver's side and, shielding my eyes, peered in. Peering out was a terrified-looking bald man of about forty. If he'd had a gun in the glovebox he'd have been pointing it right at me. Hammer cocked. 'SORRY!' I bleated and gestured with arms, now waving the toothbrush in a submissive way, in a way I hope showed low-status subservience, backing away in sky-blue dungarees. 'WRONG CAR!' I shouted a few more times before running back to my own and locking myself in. Seatbelt on. Just in case.

Mark and Liz arrived five minutes later. 'You'll never guess what happened,' I said, and gave them the edited version that made me look good rather than what really happened. Or better. They were keen to get walking and survey the lake, so after I'd packed a ton of supplies in my rucksack we set off.

Ennerdale is one of my favourite lakes. It's more like a fjord than any of the others and the lack of any dwellings or roads around its perimeter maintains the illusion that you're abroad, maybe in Austria or even Norway. Indeed, Mark told me a ranger working in Ennerdale said, 'This is the closest place to Norway in England so I work here.'

'So he likes Norway, then,' I said. Mark and Liz had both been to Norway and told me it only gets better the further north you go. I liked the idea of that and thought I would put off visiting Norway until I really had to, when I really needed a good new country to visit, one that wouldn't disappoint me by being unwild and all built-up and commercialised. Though I have never met a Norwegian with a robust sense of humour unless drunk (all the Norwegians I have known – all blokes – are weirdly macho but in a sort of fragile way: they really *hate* having the piss taken out of themselves), I have a great fondness for my imagined Norway because I feel it will be much closer to reality than, say, my imagined Atacama Desert or my imagined Amazon (which I know from Google Earth is a bit shitty, especially from Manaus onwards). When you finally visit an imagined place you've lost something, so you need some in reserve. I have Norway and the imagined city of Helsinki. Not going to either anytime soon.

We traversed a nicely made, rather Norwegian-looking, arching wooden bridge over multiple streams of a gravelly, fast-running river. 'That's a wild river,' I said. The others did not disagree. The delta of the River Liza, which fed the lake, was ribboned with fast-flowing water, creating islands that were covered in low willows and fir trees.

'This is where you could go to ground,' I said, 'if the shit hit the fan.'

'A bit damp.'

'I wonder if the river rises much?'

I pressed my case, 'No roads, plenty of fish and fresh water – what more do you want?'

'A toilet?'

I ignored this cheap gibe and outlined the general 'bug-out' plan I had been evolving in the long, dark nights after my head torch batteries had gone flat.

'The thing is, you need a place which people will overlook by virtue of it being pointless to visit. An island also allows you to see what's coming across the moat, so to speak.'

'I think you'd be better off in . . . Norway.'

The thing is, even I was not convinced about my prepping concerns for the coming decade or so. I liked the idea of being prepared and standing firm while the flimsy carapace of modern hypercapitalism cracked and splintered underfoot, yes, definitely. Like Ransome in the Russian Revolution, I smelt blood and yearned for some obscure kind of revenge on 'society', especially those aspects that seemed to impinge on things I liked and liked doing – aspects that polluted the Lake District or its nearby rivers, for example, or spread plastics into everything we ate. Boilerplate green rage, then. Except my revenge took the odd form of wanting to hide away on an island with a bow and arrow, gill net and perhaps a bag of flour or two.

Mark had some powerful binoculars, reminiscent of those a Russian sea captain might handle in the Barents Sea, and he trained them on what looked like the only island outside the delta. It was Wordsworth's by the look of it, a smattering of rocks with cormorants perching; a sub-surface island, waiting to emerge if water levels dropped.

WORDSWORTH'S ISLE IS A
SINGLE ROCK REMARKED ON IN
HIS "GUIDE TO THE LAKES" AS
"THE HAUNT OF CORMORANTS AND
SEA MEWS CLANG"

THERE ARE SEVERAL LOW HILLS THAT
ABUT THE LAKE AND AFFORD GRAND VIEWS
OF THE BIRD LIFE. BENEATH THE WATERS LURK
RARE ARCTIC CHAR. THE FJORD-LIKE SCENERY
WAS HIGHLY APPEALING AND EASIER THAN
GOING TO NORWAY...

WORDSWORTH'S ISLAND

I saw several fish rise, perhaps migratory Arctic char. Ennerdale, appropriately for its Nordic associations, has the only pure population of such fish in England, a curious anomaly trapped in lakes after the end of the Ice Age. The sea is now too warm for them. Normally, they inhabit lakes and rivers further north. Such fish mature and first migrate to the oceans between four and thirteen years of age, returning to the lakes in the summer. But the landlocked Arctic char of Ennerdale are the only ones that 'migrate' up the river to spawn, some vestigial memory still at work, whereas other Lake District char simply spawn in the lake. A cheering recent study has shown that Arctic char numbers in Ennerdale are increasing.[*]

There was a feeling that more island action was needed. We drove past Loweswater, where I had stayed in 1983 and was convinced I had rowed from Watergate farmhouse to a small island at the other end. Obviously, said island had been removed by some anti-island activist patiently digging away at the surface and scattering it in the lake, as there was no trace of it now. Mark suggested I might have misremembered but this could not have been possible. That island had gone!

---

[*] See: www.newsandstar.co.uk/news/18906405.arctic-char-populations-increase-ennerdale-water/

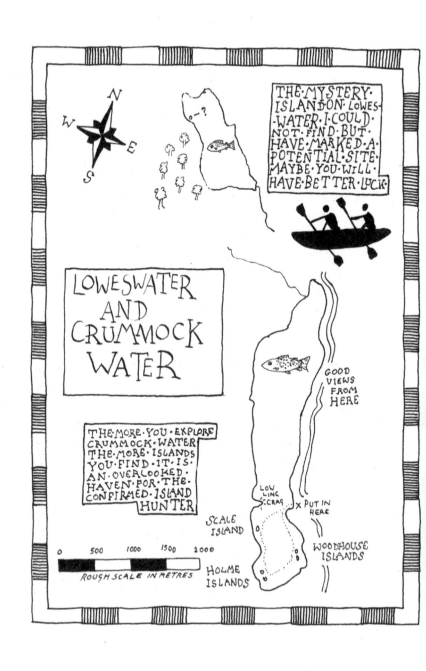

N W E S

THE·MYSTERY·
ISLAND·ON·LOWES-
·WATER·I·COULD·
NOT·FIND·BUT·
HAVE·MARKED·A·
POTENTIAL·SITE·
MAYBE·YOU·WILL·
HAVE·BETTER·LUCK·

LOWESWATER
AND
CRUMMOCK
WATER

GOOD
VIEWS
FROM
HERE

THE·MORE·YOU·EXPLORE
CRUMMOCK·WATER
THE·MORE·ISLANDS
YOU·FIND·IT·IS·
AN·OVERLOOKED·
HAVEN·FOR·THE·
CONFIRMED·ISLAND
HUNTER

LOW
LING
SCRAG

X PUT·IN
HERE

SCALE
ISLAND

WOODHOUSE
ISLANDS

0   500   1000   1500   2000

ROUGH SCALE IN METRES

HOLME
ISLANDS

And lastly Buttock Water, a small lake between Buttermere and Crummock Water.* All right, it was Crummock Water, which is another one of the wilder lakes though it does have a handy road down one side. The hills rise high and straight up from the lake edge and the three islands are obvious and pleasingly island-like.

We walked across the road and looked at the lake and looked at our watches. It was nearly 5 p.m. Mark thought I was joking when I suggested we give it a go and, on my own, I wouldn't have. But emboldened by having a boat buddy, I thought he and I should have a try.

Mark, Liz and I pumped up the boat, past the laborious phase when nothing seems to be happening through to the resistant phases where the pump shudders and makes fart noises and generally signals its discontent. We carried it over the road (moving in parallel, length on to the traffic, never cross sideways on unless you want to stop a car) and put in. Wind was about force 3, gusting force 4 – a few whitecaps but not many.

We set off paddling quite fast and I was soon knackered and begged Mark to go slower. Later, after watching us from a handy knoll, Liz remarked, 'You're not very fit, are you?' In a curious way, I was rather happy to be able to agree, because in a curious way it was a roundabout compliment to her husband and it is always both reassuring and slightly sickly sentimental to see couples long married still publicly complimentary.

_____
* This joke is one for connoisseurs; both me and my mum like it.

But I was knackered indeed – the result of no skeg, the underwater shark fin that kept the boat tracking straight (meaning much corrective paddling hard on one side or the other) and no seat back; small aids that I had till now thought superfluous – not a bit of it.

We found the first island at the eastern end of the lake. It was a rocky place with sparse vegetation. Enough room for one tent, maybe. Mark gamely held on to a bush while I clambered about and 'claimed' the place, for this is what it increasingly felt like. You stamp about, look vaguely at the limits of the island, its general features, take a few snapshots, pick up a fir cone or a feather or a leaf and mentally plant your flag: 'I claim this island for His Royal Highness . . .' Yes, it is much, much easier to steal things for other people than for yourself.

Would we try to push on to the second and third islands right over on the other side of the lake? It was getting towards dusk, and would be dark in less than an hour. 'Lakes reflect a lot of light,' said Mark, gamely, 'and there is a moon.' We set off.

The two islands took an age to reach and suddenly we were there. Both demanded inspection in the diminishing light. With big drop-offs very close to the shore, it was hard to land without plunging deep. But with Mark anchoring us I scrabbled ashore. These were small islands, forty or fifty feet long, crowned with scrub juniper, sessile oak and birch, with narrow paths made by birds and animals, but scant signs of human occupation; though, at a pinch, a single site for a tent existed on each. Mark was fond of juniper and knew a lot about it. You see less of it on moors than you did, as moor burning in the past rid us of this highly flammable bush. The wood is very springy and was used in Sweden to maintain the tension on the steel blade in bow saws. Oddly enough, Ennerdale was where we should have seen a lot, as the Old Norse word *en* means juniper and the place was named after the plants. The slightly sickening smell of gin is what I like about them, their oil, used for gin making, having been diverted from its first use as an antiseptic.

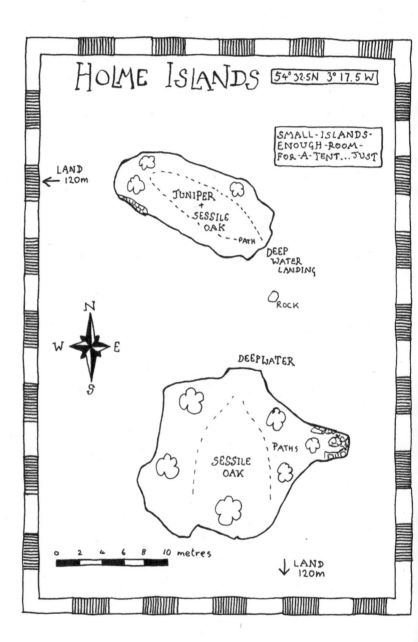

Crummock's islands were definitely less visited than those of the bigger lakes.

Now we headed back with the wind rising and the light falling, the sky in bands of blue, purple and grey as the wave tops showed white in the strange last light of the day.

Then, with darkness came the rising of the brightest moon I had yet seen in a run of bright moons. Massive, bulbous and noctilucent clouds created a cloud chamber or armchair of sorts around the bright, radiant coin of the moon. Everywhere, every fence and rising bit of stubble or rock, was silvery visible, the rippling lake like a diffraction pattern of metallic light and dark.

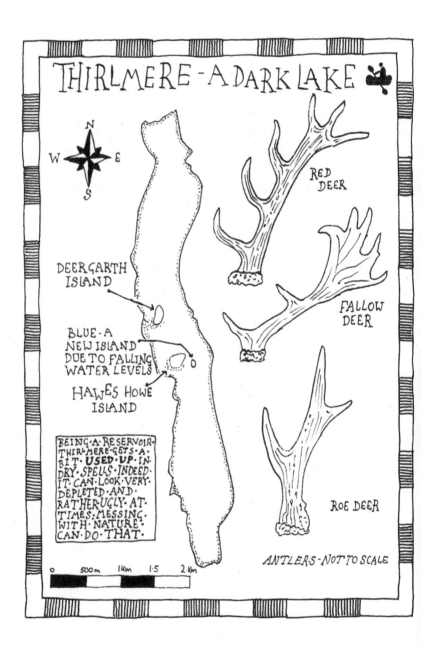

THIRLMERE - A DARK LAKE

RED DEER

FALLOW DEER

DEERGARTH ISLAND

BLUE - A NEW ISLAND DUE TO FALLING WATER LEVELS

HAWES HOWE ISLAND

BEING·A·RESERVOIR·
THIRLMERE·GETS·A·
BIT·**USED·UP**·IN·
DRY·SPELLS·INDEED·
IT·CAN·LOOK·VERY·
DEPLETED·AND·
RATHER·UGLY·AT·
TIMES·MESSING·
WITH·NATURE·
CAN·DO·THAT·

ROE DEER

0   500m   1Km   1·5   2 Km

ANTLERS - NOT TO SCALE

TEN

Rock and Paper

Lake: Thirlmere, 46 metres deep, 6.05 kilometres long, 3.27 square kilometres
Islands: Blue, Deergarth, Hawes Howe

Perched a bit above the road in a sheep-grazed carpark (no fence, so sheep cut across to find tastier bits of grass), I watched the dawn come up over Crummock Water. It was a grand, expansive feeling owing to the high ridge opposite, the steep hills on either side and the total absence of human habitation from the view.

I was getting more used to being a car nomad and certain rules of wild car camping should be noted:

1. A wide expansive view is good, excellent in fact for your mood, but less so after a night of being raked by car headlights zooming by. Especially bad are the headlights that seem to sway and then lock on like searchlights in the Blitz: they feel like eyes with a surfeit of malignant interest.
2. A cramped, hidden carpark is all right, but you won't feel like getting up in the morning. Probably means a hike to find a loo spot.

3. A carpark with a couple of other cars, preferably empty, is better than an empty one if you suspect parking overnight is forbidden.

4. When entering a carpark with cameras at night that forbids overnight parking, stop outside and drape a pair of socks over the number plate (legitimately, they could in an alternative universe be 'drying'). You will be saved the threat of deportation and/or execution from some debt-collecting company months later when you've forgotten all about it.

5. Take every opportunity to dry stuff on the roof and bonnet of the car. Damp things quickly dry there but never do when inside. If anything, they seem to get wetter . . .

6. Keep glasses and head torch on the parcel shelf; otherwise you'll roll over them during the night.

7. Resist all urges to use your Nalgene water bottle as an emergency pissoir.

It was time to face the mysteries of Thirlmere, the only other lake with islands that had been turned into a reservoir. As Ransome's mentor W.G. Collingwood put it, 'The old charm of its shores has quite vanished, and the sites of its legends are hopelessly altered, so that the walk along either side is a mere sorrow to anyone who cared for it before; the sham castles are an outrage . . .'*

Thirlmere was once rather small, and was almost two lakes separated by a very narrow waist of water. The creation of the reservoir raised the water level in stages until it was

---

* W.G. Collingwood, *The Lake Counties*, 1902 and 1932.

fifty feet higher than before. Right now, it looked to be twenty feet lower, 'drawn down' by the demands of the city. It is this constant raising and lowering of the water level that creates an ugly tideline effect on the sides of the lake, and scrubs them too, leaving a white and pinkish scoured shore.

The one thing that the flooding of the old lake by the Manchester Corporation has improved is the creation of the islands, which are the highest and most impressive of any in the Lake District. Belle Isle may be bigger and St Herbert's might rival them in terms of areas of its open and crowded woodland, but the Thirlmere islands have a rugged, Gothic grandeur of their own, rising as they do from the chasm-like depths of the lake.

To protect the lake from pollution in the reservoir's early days, swimming and boating were prohibited. This policy was supported by 'barbed wire, wire netting, regimented rows of conifers and trespass warning notices, as common as "Verboten" notices in Nazi Germany', reported the *Yorkshire Post* in 1946. They're still there in places, though now owned by the privatised United Utilities, public access is allowed to the lake's edges and it was while using such a path that I planned my assault on the three islands I could see. Closer inspection revealed that one of the islands was joined to the mainland and the third was simply a rocky islet created by the same drop in water level that had joined the other to the shore. Still, I would visit them all.

There was no one else about, no swimmers or fishermen. The lads on Derwent Water had told me Thirlmere had slim pickings for a fisherman. There was trout, pike, perch and char but not much of each, especially considering the size of the lake.

Boat pumped and loaded, I paddled off from the boulder-strewn beach. No powerboating was allowed and swimming was highly discouraged; the rain was intermittent and chilly, and the place was predictably empty. The islands rose like rock dreadnoughts from the depths, steep and high sided, impossible to land at their far ends, I paddled round and found a landing space.

This first island, Hawes Howe, like Wood Howe on Haweswater, revealed its recent creation with a dry stone wall across its middle which disappeared into the water on either side. The trees were mostly thin birches. Large Scots pines. Red mushrooms. There were fire circles in the main open zones of the island. No litter, though. In 2017, the makers, perhaps, of one of these fire circles got into such difficulties that they had to be rescued by Cumbria Fire and Rescue. The headline in the *Cumberland News* read: 'Adventurers rescued from Cumbrian island "lucky to be alive"'. A bunch of five twenty-something-year-olds had a party, and two of them decided to kayak back during the night. After capsizing, one made it to the shore and the other turned back to the island. Concern about hypothermia set in (one lad had already succumbed) and the rescue service was called. Things had become serious fast – one of the rescuers commented later: 'This could have turned from a jolly expedition to one or two fatalities but for the grace of God.' The old lesson: never split up. Especially at night when you've had a few.

The accident gave Hawes Howe a certain glamour, and at the far end, a fifty-foot-high lookout confirmed for me this was indeed a rebel king's island: *Swallows and Amazons* dragged into the territory of *Lord of the Flies*.

Of course. Why have I been missing this connection for so long? *Lord of the Flies*, the book every schoolkid in Britain has to study, along with *Animal Farm*. *Lord of the Flies*, a book that still informs my way of dividing the world into Jacks, Ralphs and Rogers. And still annoys me because it is so completely wrong.

Here's why – and it is based on my own experiences when, camped at the side of Windermere, I first glimpsed the islands that I had read about in Ransome's work. At this summer camp some of the boys wanted to be 'christened' (pegged out and daubed in rotting food as an initiation ceremony at their first summer camp) and some didn't. I was among those who had managed to avoid being christened because I was now a patrol leader and everyone assumed I had already experienced this humiliating rite. But once christened you were 'in' and you could expect the same kind of rough protection that all boys got from their patrol leaders. Scouting works because most boys are conscientious, they understand what it is to be bullied and they stop it if they see it. If they are themselves a bully, they can expect everyone to gang up on them. This isn't school where you can scarper home at night, or surround yourself with hard-nut mates or even a gang. In a Scout troop, like the boys on the island in *Lord of the Flies*, you're all in it together.

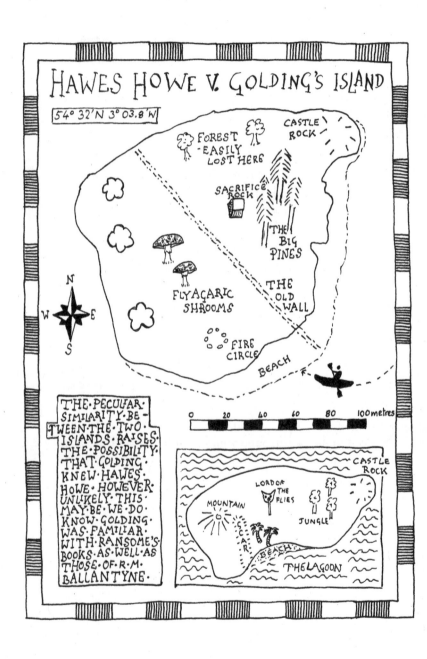

HAWES HOWE V. GOLDING'S ISLAND

54° 32'N 3° 03.8'W

FOREST -EASILY LOST HERE

CASTLE ROCK

SACRIFICE ROCK

THE BIG PINES

THE OLD WALL

FLY AGARIC SHROOMS

FIRE CIRCLE

BEACH

F

N
W · E
S

0   20   40   60   80   100 metres

THE·PECULIAR· SIMILARITY·BE- TWEEN·THE·TWO· ISLANDS·RAISES· THE·POSSIBILITY· THAT·GOLDING· KNEW·HAWES· HOWE·HOWEVER· UNLIKELY·THIS· MAY·BE·WE·DO· KNOW·GOLDING· WAS·FAMILIAR· WITH·RANSOME'S· BOOKS·AS·WELL·AS· THOSE·OF·R·M· BALLANTYNE·

CASTLE ROCK

MOUNTAIN

LORD OF THE FLIES

JUNGLE

S C A R

BEACH

THE LAGOON

Golding based his book on his experiences teaching at Bishop Wordsworth's School in Salisbury and also on presumably his own experiences as a boy; but overriding both was his wish to create an allegory about contemporary warmongering in the world. Boys who basically got on with each other and looked after each other would hardly cut it.

Hunting requires patience and skill: the characters of Piggy and Ralph would probably have become admirable hunters, working out the best way to corral and trap the wild pigs. Jack, however, becomes the boss of the hunters, so such organisation would not occur. Was Jack going to stop others from eating? That kind of gross injustice is anathema to children who perceive unfairness more strongly than adults do. Jack would simply not have been followed even if he was the biggest and strongest: the leader among boys is always the most popular, not the toughest. Anyone who has known serious bullies knows they are always isolated figures, usually with just one, or at most two, feeble hangers-on. So even if Jack had been the best hunter he'd have to be part of the overall workings of the tribe, which would have been run by Ralph. Good guys win except in bureaucracies, where bad guys with more energy do all the boring jobs and thus gain power of the organisation. This doesn't happen in a tribe where an alliance of the popular and the clever rule the roost.

Ah yes, but what if there are psychopaths like Roger and Jack at the top? Well, unless they have a sense of humour they'll be ostracised. The element missing from Golding's book, glaringly missing, is the love of larking about and humour that children have. There would be a class clown or wit, there always is, who would slyly take the piss out of the bullies behind their backs, thus reducing their appeal. The good guys – those with a proper sense of humour – would side with the wits to dominate proceedings. The boys would have grown up fast and run the island very well indeed.

Maybe an island like this one. I found a giant rock in the middle of a clearing, good for a human sacrifice. Islands get you thinking like that, because the inhabitants of islands in the South Seas could well be cannibals, if you're imprinted as I am by the exploits of Cook and Bligh refracted through the children's books of Marryat, Ballantyne, Forester and Ransome.

Another red and white shroom – a fly agaric. They are everywhere on the Thirlmere islands. Said to be the inspiration for Santa's red and white costume, the fly agaric is the hallucinogen of choice among the reindeer of Lapland and Siberia. Naturally humans have learnt from their beasts and by drinking reindeer urine you can get quite a high. Less a strict hallucinogen than something that promotes a trance-like state in which the world seems strange, with dreams of incredible vivacity, the fly agaric affects people in different ways, though is rarely fatal in microdoses. Of course, anyone who faffs with mushrooms is a braver (or more foolhardy) soul than I, and I simply admired its startling colours and moved on. Ever since reading that shamans insist that some people take inner journeys to learn (including mushroom-inspired dreams) while others need to make real journeys, and once you have started with the real journeys you are bound by that method, I have left the dream journeying to others.

I left Hawes Howe island for another, a new island I called
'Blue'. It was a whale-like rising of smooth rock, no, make
that liver-like: the skeined and tegumental liver fresh from
the innards of a dead giant. 'Blue' rose in the middle of the
lake; I could tell by the scummy water line along this rock
island's edge, that it was usually almost completely submerged. But now it was a great beast in its own right, slippery
and grey.

Wedging the rope round a rock at its base, I climbed up
one side. This felt like quite an achievement despite it being
only about fifteen feet. At the top were two pebbles poorly
balanced on each other. I was not the first arrival. But I could
improve on this cairn. At Wigtown Book Festival I'd learnt
from a Dutch sculptor how to balance stones in the craziest
way possible. The key is to find three points of contact that
stand out on any one surface. These form a triangle of support for that stone wherever they are located on it – which
could be on the smallest plane rather than, as you'd imagine,
on the biggest and flattest-looking surface. Instead of piling
stones up like a sandwich, you can balance them upright to
make a stone tower five or six rocks high. Which I now did.
It may even still be there.

The final island, Deergarth, was another people camped
on; in the main clearing was a big stone ring filled with
broken and half-melted Peroni, Jack Daniel's and Carlsberg
bottles, along with bits of plastic and rusted barbecue grills.
All around, the trees were shorn of their lower branches and
a couple of pines were simply hacked stumps. You get lazy
looking for wood when you're pissed and it's night-time.

At least the litter wasn't dispersed. It had all been corralled
into this one ugly little spot. The rupturing bin liners of

litter you see left at lay-bys by camper wagoneers, who can't be arsed to find a proper bin, are worse, really. When you have a vehicle your capacity for damaging the environment increases exponentially. These island pirates had to hike in their bottles of Jack and their axes and saws, and that limited them a lot. But a car can carry a ton of rubbish, which can be left anywhere. And a chainsaw fits into a car boot rather easier than a rucksack does.

The best thing conservationists can do is to ban cars from getting to places that they wish to preserve. The idea behind creating more carparks and better road access to the Lake District is insane. Make it harder to get there, except by walking. Maybe have a few mega carparks in the towns and that's it. The Lake District towns have always been good at hoovering up vast crowds of trippers, and did so even in Ransome's day – and that's where they should stay. I am a confirmed elitist when it comes to places as fragile and near to vast populations as the Lakes are: only those who earn their way through walking (or paddling) should be allowed. I'd be all for a cycling-only policy along many of the roads (with the mega park and ride (a bike) carparks I have mentioned earlier flanking the motorway at Penrith).

In another part of the island, I came across a clearing of old Scots pine trees where the reddish trunks had fallen in a random fashion – as if a giant playing Jenga had carelessly lost the game. The Scots pine is among my favourite trees, the only pine native to the UK. It was once used to make such utilitarian things as telegraph poles and railway sleepers; when dipped in creosote, Scots pine wood lasts forever, almost. Originally, it would have been called 'fir', an old

English word linked to the Danish *fyr* and the German *Fohre* and *Kiefer*,* as well as the Norse *furu*. The link between pine and fire, fir and fire, is obvious. And Scots pine wood makes an excellent fuel. Trees and fire, Norsemen and Teutons lurking in their forest, watching their fires, waiting until dawn.

Making my way back from the clearing, I lost my way and simply had to keep going until I reached the water's edge. I now knew where I was from the view of the lake. If I had been really lost, I could then have worked my way around the perimeter of the island. It struck me that there is a certain point – a certain size and, to a lesser extent, shape of island – that allows you to get lost on it; and this island was just about big enough. Most of the others weren't. Interestingly, even on fairly small Peel Island I had managed to lose my way for a moment or two since it is divided in two with the wilder part hidden from the dip which is pleasantly open with its worn close grass.

The getting lost point is close to the Robinson Crusoe moment, which I experienced on Wood Howe: a place big enough for you *not to recall* a footprint you have made. But it's more than that; it's the lack of confidence, the self-doubt that grows when you know you are alone on an island. All of life can be seen as a to-and-fro between interest and existential confidence, the self-belief in one's rightness but also one's right to be *here*, in this place. Sometimes I was trespassing with a spring in my step, a cocky belief in my right to roam *anywhere*. At other times, I was slinking about

---

* *Kiefer* can mean either 'pine' or 'jaw'. Not sure which Kiefer Sutherland is named after.

like a nervous cat that knows it isn't welcome. What made the difference? Why was one place conducive to existential confidence while another drained it away?

Perhaps *being interested* is the answer. Being interested (which always threatens to topple over into sexual interest or at least *looks* similar) is something that drives one into involvement with that thing; it can also make one into a voyeur, or a collector. Collecting mania is one way of characterising attachment – and the stronger it is, the more moved we are to act, again it serves to make *life* happen. Being *interested* is also connected to existential self-confidence (I use this cumbersome term to differentiate it from mere ordinary confidence, which is an outer condition, a set of learnt behaviours that project a certain kind of appearance). A great interest appears to *inflate* the inner world in some sense; it sharpens all other interests too. This burgeoning sense of inner confidence is what the young seek when they talk about 'becoming more confident'. And, of course, when you have existential self-confidence, you encounter a more interesting version of life. You come across what you are looking for – partly because you are looking harder, which again feeds back into the interest. Without interests, which could simply be the nurturing of a secret close to one's heart (one could easily imagine a prisoner doing this, holding that one dear thing to themselves as a bulwark against the hostility and deprivation of a jail cell), we are without existential self-confidence.

When the island is so small that you cannot be lost on it, it becomes you – an extension of yourself, almost an extension of a limb or a hand. The island is subsumed by the self, and your sense of existing is strengthened. This is the meaning of retiring to an island. Or of running to an island when some terrible breakdown of society happens. You become the island.

But when the island is bigger, and the kind you can get lost on, a more subtle change occurs. You become the explorer, the hunter, the one who will become the owner of the island. Your interest is piqued, it grows all the time, until you find the fatal footprint that punctures your ambitions to be alone.

This whole trip, with its absurd interludes of dossing in a car and finding 'safe' places to camp, interspersed with outings to all kinds of island, was a severe test of my existential self-confidence, however humorous that may sound.* It really drained me to be going again and again to these places that would either become a part of me, or require minute exploration so that they could be collected and owned in some way. I have always felt ownership was decided by the seriousness and intensity of the gaze and not mere title deed, which is why a landscape is owned by those who admire its views rather than the duffer who pays the mortgage. It is a strange opinion to have, I admit, yet you need only spend a small amount of time in places of great grandeur such as mountains and vast deserts, and it becomes quite obviously truer than the materialist fantasy on which the whole of modern Western economics is based. The great Tolstoy story 'How Much Land Does a Man Need?'† informs us of the older view of land: that it could be occupied but never owned.

---

* Monty Python did for the word *existential* and *existentialist* what Marlon Brando did for butter.
† Six foot by three foot. Work it out.

Anyway, those old pines seemed to me to have been planted in the diagonal fashion known as the quincunx, which Sir Thomas Browne, in one of the most extraordinary essays in English, attributed to the original planting of the Garden of Eden. The trouble with the quincunx is that once you see one, you start to see the same pattern everywhere. And now that I could see it here too, it confirmed my intuition that all islands are in some sense Eden. Or, that on arriving on them, we expect to find our own Eden, as Ransome did with Wild Cat Island and, later, with Trindade Island in *Peter Duck*.

You can't return to Eden; the very act of 'seeing if it has changed' spoils things. So we hope that the next place we arrive at will be a new Eden. By Eden, I mean the perfect place for us, a physical equivalent to the perfect job or the perfect partner. It seems our *right*. Or something we should definitely hold out for.

By going to these islands, I had created a machine for generating Edens, three or four a day. Surprisingly, those that seemed most like Eden were the tiniest ones, with a single tree and only enough space to curl up in.

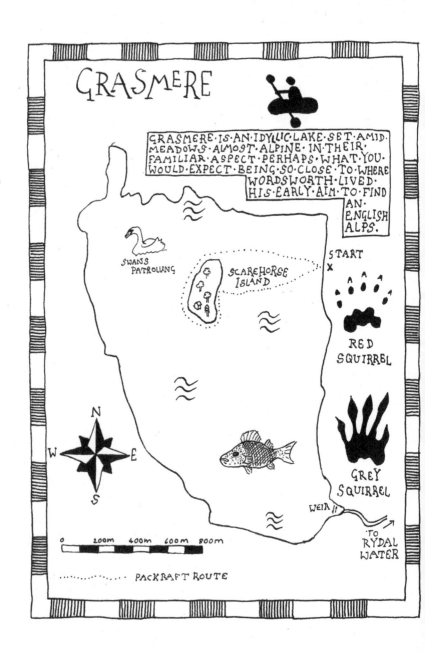

GRASMERE

GRASMERE·IS·AN·IDYLLIC·LAKE·SET·AMID·
MEADOWS·ALMOST·ALPINE·IN·THEIR·
FAMILIAR·ASPECT·PERHAPS·WHAT·YOU·
WOULD·EXPECT·BEING·SO·CLOSE·TO·WHERE
WORDSWORTH·LIVED·
HIS·EARLY·AIM·TO·FIND·
AN·
ENGLISH·
ALPS.

SWANS
PATROLLING

SCAREHORSE
ISLAND

START
X

RED
SQUIRREL

GREY
SQUIRREL

N
W   E
S

WEIR

TO
RYDAL
WATER

0   200m 400m 600m 800m

·············· PACKRAFT ROUTE

ELEVEN

An Island Is an Island

Lake: Grasmere, 21 metres deep, 1.54 kilometres long, 0.62 square kilometres
Island: Scarehorse House / Grasmere Island

'Grasmere, Rydal Water, Eltermere – almost done,' I said to myself, and then realised it would have to be back to Windermere for two more islands that could not be left undone. The island journey, though, was just warming up, or so I felt; I was just getting into the swing of it, becoming slicker at mounting my amphibious assaults.

Grasmere, then. The most 'Lake District' of all the lakes. No wonder Wordsworth lived here. Grass sward comes down to the lake. There is a perfect rough-hewn mini mountain in front of the village, with an alpine feel that Dorothy Wordsworth noted two centuries ago. There are well-proportioned hills beyond. I've mentioned Wordsworth's view on islands before, and it was around his time that people began to buy them up and live on some of them. No doubt the nature poets had 'added value' to this rural real estate.

DISSIMULATING

Baudrillard, another philosopher I have lasting affection for, if only because he was also a tentative artist, famously ascribed four ways to state an object's value. According to these, an island has functional value (such as a place to hide during the coming economic apocalypse). It has a market value (recently, an island on Derwent Water went up for rent at £40,000 a year). It has symbolic value (an island is a place of exclusion and retreat). And there is its 'sign value' too (every multimillionaire thinks about getting one, surely). Owning an island, or, second best, a property on an island, is how you align yourself with the privileged and wealthy.

But I'd add a fifth value to those soundly observed other four: the mystical or perhaps magical or simply unconscious (deeply mysterious to most) value of an island. When the children in Arthur Ransome's *Swallows and Amazons* go to the island, it is because the place is of magical significance; it functions like an enchanted forest in a Russian fairy tale, Russia being of course where Ransome spent his early career (in between playing chess with Lenin and marrying Trotsky's secretary) translating and publishing.

Vladimir Propp, the Soviet folklorist who identified from Russian fairy tales (some of the very same that Ransome translated) the narrative trajectory that would later become known as 'the hero's journey', realised that along with dreams and childhood we can interrogate the fairy tale for useful information about our own destiny. In fact, one might say the vast repertoire of fairy tales, which Propp boiled down to thirty-one *operations*, amounts to multiple insights into human destiny.

Research indicates that the oldest fairy tale, 'The Smith and the Devil', is over 6,000 years old.* 'Beauty and the Beast' is over 4,000 years old, 'Rumpelstiltskin' 5,000 . . . These tales for children encode our ideas of destiny; they might be, in fact, a rather useful roadmap. Certainly, the Sufis think so: the ancient Sufi story 'The Islanders' is presented as a fairy story but very much designed to teach us something.

But the repetition of fairy tales is designed to teach in a different way to classroom lectures. They work insidiously, indirectly, by imprinting a pattern on our subconscious.† In *Swallows and Amazons*, the children *have* to go to the island: it is, in the parlance of Propp and later story analysts, an initiating event. Without the island there would be no story. (And without Kirrin Island, there'd be no Famous Five.) The island and, more specifically, the going to the island is perhaps a metaphorical act – a symbolic value in Baudrillard's schema – but also a mystical one, a magical one.

I feel this in a concentrated, fleeting form as I approach any new island. They have a symbolic value for me as a way of honouring exploration: an uninhabited island always demands to be explored, quite unlike an uninhabited park or field. An island suggests the minimum needed for human survival; it's the basic unit of being a human – cut off from his usual tribe he will still survive. Hence my identification

* Dr Jamie Tehrani, 'Comparative Phylogenetic Analyses' 2016, University of Durham/Royal Society Open Science paper.
† The semi-subterranean clearing house of the unconscious.

of the reservoir island as the ultimate 'bunker'. Blyton and Ransome played their part in shaping my view, but so did watching the French-German TV series *Robinson Crusoe*. Made in the mid-1960s, it's as old as I am. (And worth finding on YouTube if only for the mesmeric theme tune.)

Blyton's greatest creation, Kirrin Island (whose profile can be discerned in Corfe Castle: Blyton wrote many of her novels while staying in the nearby Knoll House Hotel), is of course a treasure island, one with underground structures as well as a wreck. It is the distilled essence of island and as potent as any drug. Ransome's islands, like those of the Lake District itself, are less intense in function. One might be a treasure island but it is a sort of comedy treasure. If anything, there is something too prosaic about his depicted islands, yet they are the stronger for it. It is some great kind of secret that the gentler and less impressive the external form the longer it lasts, and the more lasting and powerful occupancy of our souls it commands. And by soul, I mean that suspected permanency we carry around that looks to childhood for its pointers and orientation.

For it is true that we calibrate our lives by how they do or don't measure up to childhood dreams. We develop workarounds, like the Ptolemaic astronomers who could more accurately predict the planets' positions than later Copernican ones despite using a wrong model, a wrong map. Maps, islands, childhood – we are getting somewhere. So even if our initial fantastical notions about life are completely wrong, the fact of being in the world means we adapt and get on with things. But that early fantasy (which Freud boringly ascribes solely to sexual urges of various kinds) remains, waiting to break out when we least expect it.

No man is an island entire of itself – and isn't life a process of discovering that either too early or a little late? We are always arriving at islands at dusk and underprepared; who can forget, once seen, the Swiss Symbolist artist Böcklin's *The Isle of the Dead*?

The island is always a place where one is reborn: Crusoe is in fiction and the man who was the real-life inspiration for him, Alexander Selkirk, was reported to be utterly adapted to life on the Juan Fernández Islands, so much so the sailors on his rescuing ship were astonished at his barefooted agility and strength (which of course waned as the voyage neared England). The island is a place where you discover your real self, the real me. Ibn Tufail's classic *Ḥayy ibn Yaqẓān*, the world's first psychological novel, posits the thought experiment of a man who is washed up on a desert island as a child and how he develops his notion of truth and comes to understand the world around him.* In a way, it's like a more contextualised and sensible version of Descartes' later thought experiment of doubting everything except the thought he is having. But since a thought presupposes a human thinker and a human needs a life-support system for his body as well as his mind, then a deserted island as the minimal state makes more sense as a starting point for philosophical excursions.

A child alone on a desert island. Maybe all that Blyton and Ransome were doing (not to mention the film *The Blue Lagoon*) was tapping into some essential feature of our mind's structure. That 'going to the island' is what we are doing all our lives.

---

* This book is the most translated text in Arabic after the Quran and *One Thousand and One Nights*.

There is a wonderful story that starts and configures to a great extent the seminal work by Idries Shah, *The Sufis*. Mentioned briefly earlier, 'The Islanders' is a fairy tale that speaks of a people who have forgotten how to swim and build ships, who must nevertheless leave their current island for another. Their difficulty is that not only have they forgotten their aquatic skills, but they have developed comforting notions that deny the possibility that such skills even exist.

The island is a place where you learn how to get to other islands. Perhaps you will swim, perhaps you will use a boat. The island is where you go to escape the 'they' world and to make your own world, a new life, on a truer level of existence. The 'they' world is when you are powerless, alone, watching the news or scrolling through Facebook, getting alternately angry and sad at things over which you have no control that are the fault of 'them', 'the government', 'big business' 'the system'. I must spend half my life in the 'they' world sometimes. It thrives on lack of activity and connection, which is why old people and isolated twenty-somethings get sucked into it, or can do. When we are on a trip looking for islands, the 'they' world magically begins to shrink. We enter our world. Now I see the desire to blame 'them' not as something to try to shut down or forcibly ignore; rather, it is a useful warning that my life is currently off course. Get outside, get in a boat, look for an island: this is what it means.

Parking, again.

Grasmere has parking. No problem, lay-by right by the main road that runs out of Grasmere village which is thronging with Wordsworthy tourists – give that a miss for a start. Unload the boat. Connoisseur that I was, I figured the packraft would be more than adequate for the relatively flat surface of the lake.

There are herons nesting on Grasmere Island and I saw a huge one coasting in like something designed with stealth capabilities. It is not surprising as the lake has more than its average share of trout, pike and perch.

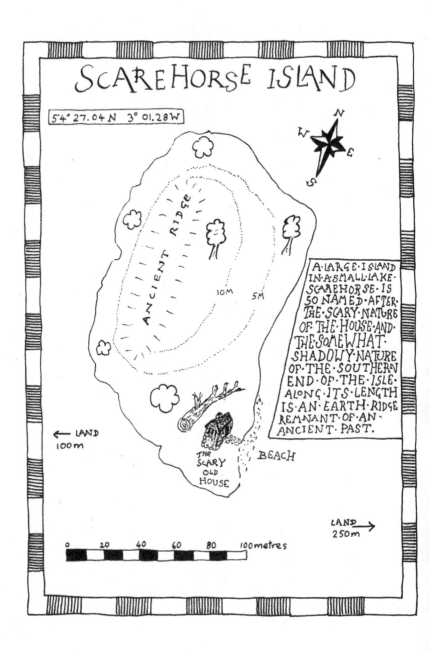

SCAREHORSE ISLAND

54° 27.04 N 3° 01.28 W

A LARGE ISLAND IN A SMALL LAKE SCAREHORSE IS SO NAMED AFTER THE SCARY NATURE OF THE HOUSE AND THE SOMEWHAT SHADOWY NATURE OF THE SOUTHERN END OF THE ISLE. ALONG ITS LENGTH IS AN EARTH RIDGE REMNANT OF AN ANCIENT PAST.

ANCIENT RIDGE

10M   5M

← LAND 100m

THE SCARY OLD HOUSE

BEACH

LAND → 250m

0   20   40   60   80   100 metres

On the island, there was a huge bank, brown with beech leaves. I climbed up and followed it down to the end, where a semi-ruined, bothy-like habitation stood. This, I felt, was like the stable for a ghost animal, a haunting horse rather than a haunted house – the scarehorse. So this became my name for the island too. Dank and dark inside with open slit-holes for windows, it was the sort of place you'd be grateful for only if it was raining hard. A smell of old fires. Wood, neatly chopped, spoke of people who came here regularly. The island, only relatively recently donated to the National Trust, had in fact, with its sale into private hands in 1893, been one of the examples of things that needed preserving, but couldn't be. Until now.

The National Trust. More benign than a national park with its 'rangers'. Better than the Forestry Commission with its hard-hatted chainsawyers. Better than a utility company and way better than a corporation with its security firm. No, the lowest form of life that gains control of beauty spots has to be film and TV companies that employ 'security' to boss and bully normal people who happen to be walking by. Never give permission ever to one of these parasites! The National Trust still has a benign feel, though no doubt like all big organisations it could topple into fascistic authoritarianism very easily . . .

There is a famous ancient oak tree on Scarehorse Island, which was there in Wordsworth's day. Now surrounded by other trees, somewhat reduced, it is in its cracked and ample glory like a seething bag of snakes, its limbs extruding everywhere. Oaks, like islands, need a lot of water – 100 gallons a day or more – and the damp land here is perfect.

The two kinds of native oak can be found on most of the islands. The one on Grasmere is a pedunculate oak, less tall than the sessile oak, which with its extensive trunk is more useful as a timber provider. You can tell the difference between them from the stalkless acorns but well-stalked leaves on the sessile oak, whereas *Quercus robur*, the pedunculate oak, has stalked acorns and stalkless leaves.

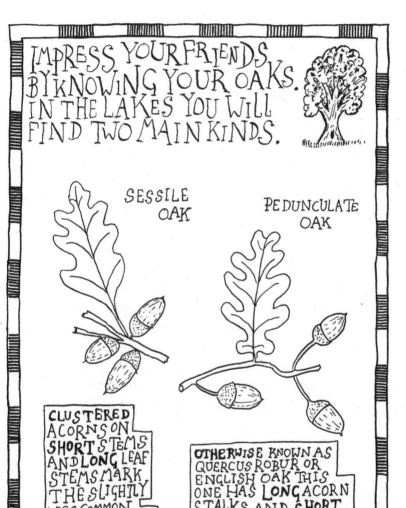

IMPRESS YOUR FRIENDS BY KNOWING YOUR OAKS. IN THE LAKES YOU WILL FIND TWO MAIN KINDS.

SESSILE OAK

PEDUNCULATE OAK

CLUSTERED ACORNS ON **SHORT** STEMS AND **LONG** LEAF STEMS MARK THE SLIGHTLY LESS COMMON SESSILE OAK

OTHERWISE KNOWN AS QUERCUS ROBUR OR ENGLISH OAK THIS ONE HAS **LONG** ACORN STALKS AND **SHORT** LEAF STALKS PLUS TWO SMALL LOBES AT THE LEAF BASE.

Oak likes a temperate climate. In Norway, it only grows in the south, and since it is the main wood of the Viking craft it confirms that the main forces of raiders didn't come from those frozen fjords but from the warmer valleys nearer Denmark. Oak is, like the Viking, an aggressive coloniser: it will establish itself on any pasture left untended. Probably due to the denudation of British oaks for ships, charcoal and building, we have come to think of it as rare and perhaps hard to grow. But, as a whole, oaks constitute nearly a fifth of all British trees and with a continued emphasis on broad leaf over conifer planting that will increase.

I left the island and got caught in crosswinds. The lake now had a thousand dimples patterning its surface as the waves at cross purposes cancelled or amplified each other. Pitter-pattering and threatening to upset my cockleshell of a boat. Then, clear of that, I was swum at by two swans, with their wraparound shades and down-slanted sneers, but using a paddle slap I manfully drove them away.

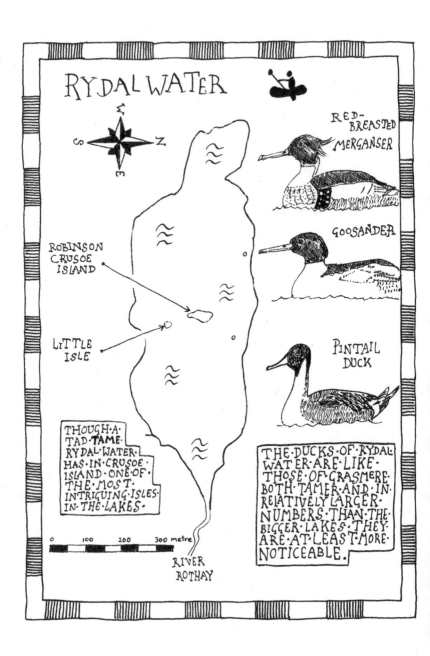

RYDAL WATER

RED-BREASTED MERGANSER

GOOSANDER

PINTAIL DUCK

ROBINSON CRUSOE ISLAND

LITTLE ISLE

THOUGH·A· TAD·**TAME·** RYDAL·WATER· HAS·IN·CRUSOE· ISLAND·ONE·OF· THE·MOST· INTRIGUING·ISLES· IN·THE·LAKES·

0   100   200   300 metre

RIVER ROTHAY

THE·DUCKS·OF·RYDAL· WATER·ARE·LIKE· THOSE·OF·GRASMERE· BOTH·TAMER·AND·IN· RELATIVELY·LARGER· NUMBERS·THAN·THE· BIGGER·LAKES·THEY· ARE·AT·LEAST·MORE· NOTICEABLE.

TWELVE

Crusoe

Lake: Rydal Water, 17 metres deep, 1.18 kilometres long, 0.31 square kilometres
Islands: Oak Island, Magners Isle, Stairway to Heaven Island, Crusoe Island

Parking was becoming not just *a* problem but *the* problem. A fancy carpark at the end of Rydal Water was duly paid for despite the £7.20-for-two-hours price tag. Of course, this is entirely justified on one level. Keep the punters in their despoiling cars out. But rich folk think nothing of hefty parking fees, tis the poor who find it raw. So, again, have huge free carparks miles out and make us walk or cycle in. Those who cannot walk could use wheelchairs. But would we allow electric ones? And electric bikes? It isn't easy being a world leader and deciding such things . . .

Two kids in front of the carpark machine (not entirely unaware that I was behind and listening) were muttering, 'We need to open this up' and 'I've found where the money is.' They both fiddled with the stark battleship-grey lump of metal. 'If we open this up we can be millionaires . . .' But the older one had already left and his brother with the big plans had no choice but to trail after him.

The signs: not good. It seems no canoes, no kayaks and no paddleboards are allowed on this lake – but you can *swim*! Squirming as per usual in the face of 'The Man', and cognisant of the wonderful English legal principle (oft forgot) that anything not specifically forbidden is allowed, I remind myself I do not have a kayak or a canoe but a *packraft*.

The kit was already in my rucksack, including the paddle. Ready to deploy at a moment's notice. Rydal Water is distant from the road by virtue of verdant albeit soggy fields full of cows and sheep. A guesthouse overlooks the four islands, which includes the two main ones and two that are much, much smaller. In fact, one was so small it ranked as the smallest island in the Lake District that wasn't a stone poking through the water.

It was this mini island I chose to wade to (togged up as I was in the carpark with my Neoprene stockingfoot waders, which look like slightly rubbery trousers). The gap across was only ten feet, maybe less. The depth of the water was above knee height, maybe up to the waist if you weren't careful, as underfoot was very uneven with rocks. A swimmer would have swum but I'm a wader by nature. And when you're in waders the pleasure of knowing you are unlikely to get wet is high. You set off from the bank without trepidation (as you do in rolled-up trousers) but brimful of confidence. Having these protective waders changes the nature of the medium. The water is no longer a fear-inducing enemy. It becomes more interesting because it is something you aren't trying to keep out of.

The lake itself was small, really, compared to the giant expanses of Ullswater and Windermere. Here, the valley that has pinched off Grasmere and Rydal Water is on a smaller scale. Both lakes are fed by the River Rothay. Rydal Water is not long. You can see the whole of it from any spot on the bank, which is a measure of its diminutive size. It is not especially deep, either.

Bagging the small island was a nice start to things; and it was delightfully small – perfect, even. It had its own small share of hard-won earth as well as rock. There was even a single spindly tree, an oak. You could, if curled up, sleep here at a pinch. A good place to bury treasure. I named it Oak Island.

But it was no use to hide out on.

The rain was pitter-pattering down now and the clouds had lowered to the surrounding hills. This was the Lake District weather I remembered from many excursions and climbing trips: the unabashed abundance of wet sky, sky fall of rain and soggy mist. Quite like it really, as long as there is a warm change of clothes somewhere in the background. Or a pub.

But blowing up boats in the rain is a pain. All your kit patiently waiting for you to finish the task also gets wet. And the contortions of moving around the inflating boat expose you to rain in ways you wouldn't be if you were stately and upright. Also, I notice I am visible from Nab Cottage, former residence of the opium addict Thomas De Quincey and later Coleridge's slightly feckless but charming son Hartley, who died here in William Wordsworth's arms, and who considered his time here wasted in 'the woeful impotence of weak resolve'. A sad place, then, with its opium dreamer connections (now a B&B and international language school), yet I am not surprised by the connections: walking releases its own natural opiates and old smack addicts are known to cure themselves with long walks heaven knows where. And where better to walk than the Lake District? Unless you prefer boating.

I found a large oak to hide under and keep out of the rain while I inflated Bertha. Yes, it was this late in the game when I finally came up with a name for the packraft. Bertha suggested to me a naughty postcard from the 1930s, one with swimwear-clad people who looked inflatable, often with rubber rings, on English beaches. The packraft, with its jaunty black and yellow colouring and bulbous lines, was a real Bertha.

Once she was inflated, I carried Bertha to the water's edge, which was somewhat indistinct owing to reeds. I found a place where I could set off, and because I had not got a heavy rucksack, paddling out was rather easy and enjoyable.

Small lakes are stiller than big lakes. Indeed, there is a mathematical relationship between wave size and lake size. Being less exposed, small lakes are usually less windy too. Small lakes are more like ponds – Rydal and Grasmere certainly are, and paddling in a toy-like boat on a pond has something of the model village about it. Roaming through Legoland, land of the giants. The manicured countryside around the lake adds to this feeling, but the first island I got to, much smaller than the other two (maybe ten metres long) was as wild as can be. Once I had battled through some shoreside elders, I had to fight my way past brambles to make it to the large, fin-like rock at the centre of the island.

The place was really overgrown, full of rocks. I had to

wriggle to get through. But surely overgrown is the wrong term? This was an island too small to use for anything, yet it had failed to achieve the equilibrium state of undisturbed nature in which large trees block out light, thus opening up the lower areas, eventually, to grass or low foliage. Here the fight was still on. The trees – holly, oak, alder – were all fighting the brambly undergrowth and the liberally strewn rocks. It felt as if the island had been cleared maybe thirty or forty years ago and this was all secondary growth. These are the sort of places you encounter in remote, but logged, wilderness. Nature is wilder here than elsewhere, as if it's making up for lost time, overeager to fill the vacuum of depleted flora. You feel the aggression and ugliness of nature you find in mudslides and rock falls, in wild rivers after a storm, or the boulder-strewn shore locked tight with mangled driftwood freshly bitten off by the powerful wind and the heavy current. Such places are certainly not beautiful unless you zoom in, exclude the wide angle and find the microcosm.

No path, nowhere to camp, but there, on the large rock in the middle of the island, a single corroded Magners cider can, evidence of European explorers who had beaten me to it.

The first big island (known locally as Little Isle) had a partially submerged stone slipway that mesmerised me from far off. It had such an ancient and useful look, such a casual utility but was crafted from such heavy stone slabs, that I thought of this as the stairway to heaven. I could imagine swimmers gliding up to these slabs and slowly emerging from the magical lake that then and there took on the appearance of an Arthurian legend right out of a Burne-Jones painting.

Somewhere in this lake would be Excalibur, for sure. And, if I arrived early enough, the milkweed- and anemone-strewn Lady of the Lake would be there too, combing her hair.

I love things made of stone that are massive beyond requirement, indicative of vast months of human toil. I once found a giant tank in the Peak District carved entirely from a single massive block of gritstone, which was especially pleasing as it spoke of a previous era where time ran so slowly through people's hands; I mean the psychological sense of time passing, which is connected in some ways to how closely we engage with life. I admire the way they engaged with useful tasks, but what I envy is the deceleration of time passing, something I have to find on a trip like this. Island hopping slows time right down. A day can seem like a week does in the ordinary world of laptops and lattes.

The slipway, when Bertha finally bumbled up to it, was indeed well made, the large square flags carefully laid a hundred or more years ago I guess. It was clearly an island used to being visited, and had been for very many years, grassy, wide open with oaks and pines. It was perhaps about seventy metres in length, though I didn't pace it. My attention was immediately drawn to a roofless hut that looked like a sheep enclosure, which stood at the far end of the island. It had a bitten-out hole in the upper wall: the remains of a window, plus a doorway. It was a place good for crouching in, out of the wind. Crouching is a pleasurable activity in its own right, allied with squeezing into small places, through railings, preferably impossibly narrow-looking. It belongs to the arts of escape needed only by children and by adventurers – the people who have professionalised, to some extent, the play aspect of exploration that all children love.

I wasn't sure whether to have my brew in the crouching hut or out in the open, where a log had 'seats' made from artfully arranged slates along its length. There was the usual fireplace made from flat stones. The first instinct is always to make a fire.

I compromised by crouching down over the flimsy stove at the edge of the fireplace. How many more brews before I finished my island hopping excursion? At first I had imagined it would be like the Burt Lancaster film *The Swimmer*, where a Connecticut Yankee swims his way home across the suburban pools belonging to his neighbours.* The film ends up being depressing because we realise that instead of being a jaunty passage through suburbia, thumbing its nose at the bourgeoisie, it's actually the portrait of someone going mad; and this micro adventure, instead of being an example of sanity in a mad world, is an example of madness in a mad world. *Nein, danke*, I like my myths light. But the idea is superb, as Roger Deakin's book *Waterlog* showed: making a journey through connected swims is like becoming amphibious, surely an unconscious dream for any species that originated in the sea?

So the idea of being an amphibian was ditched in favour of having a boat, which immediately gave a graver note to the whole enterprise – more Charon, the ferryman of the dead, crossing the Styx than splashing around in a paddling pool. At least it had felt like that at times, and now I was getting closer to the end I was encouraged again to think about my idea of the fork in life and where that fitted into this journey.

On a journey that involves things like crouching and

---

* The film is based on the John Cheever short story of the same name.

hiding, you are forced back to an earlier stage. It may be painful or even humiliating but at the same time new thoughts are liberated. You are breaking the pattern, getting out of the rut. And what I now saw is that your *whole* life, your context, your home and work existence *is* the rut. Never mind your regular habits and the things you do routinely. All that is simply additional gunk. If you try to enforce extra routines on top of a regular life, you risk going the wrong way at the fork.

I don't mean your regular life should be chaotic. I mean it should be organised so that you have plenty of space to get what you want done, but if someone interrupts you you don't have to shut them out. I think of people I know with insane routines of early morning exercise, followed by hours of work and scheduled free time, with every minute blocked out and accounted for. It's not just a rut, it's a canyon, a slit trench, a grave. It's not that I don't understand it, I do, I've been there myself many times. It's a *reaction* to the fast pace of change the mechanical life forces on us. One minute you're a journalist with an expense account, the next minute you're a penniless 'writer' with a Twitter account. Shit doesn't just happen, it happens *fast*. And shit is happening everywhere, twenty-four hours a day, anytime you care to log on, which is all the time in my case if I'm not careful.

So you make a choice. Enough's enough. I will build my own fortress of calm, my own palace of perfect routine. I will conquer the world by outrunning it, getting up earlier, eating better, timing myself . . . It's not the self-improvement that's wrong, it's the attempt to disconnect, to run scared – earphones in, music on, sunglasses and smart watch primed . . . The attempt to control everything is a reaction, I am sure, to the spectacle of utter chaos which is the internet version of reality. By getting clear of it, heading to an island – a real island of calm – I had glimpsed something: choose the change you want to be a part of. Don't confuse *more information* with real change. Hiding from information is OK but don't hide from it in 'routine'. Instead of becoming more rigid every year – so rigid you take the wrong fork – learn to bend some more each year, discover new levels of mental flexibility, living flexibility; 'embrace change' is easy to say, but you can start by liking changes in your friends, their growth and development. You know someone has taken a wrong turn when they wail, 'You never used to do that' . . . Look out for small changes in the way they dress and speak, and applaud them; the Buddha nature of reality is not more information, it is change.

I was coming to see that 'routines'* should only be employed on journeys, or to get a specific job done. They must always be temporary. Otherwise some kind of dreadful ossification sets in. You start losing your sense of humour. You're surviving all right, but that's it. Instead, submit to your environment – that is routine enough – while becoming ever more open to it, interested . . . In between all the living, remain open to its essential humour; there is a clue there too.

Two ducks approached Bertha at the water's edge: red-breasted mergansers with their joke-tufty heads, a more humorous-looking bird, I note, than a mallard or shelduck.

---

* I am aware I may be misunderstood here, despite my explanations above. My meaning is: good routine – a temporary thing to achieve a specific goal. Bad routine – a permanent way of doing things because you fear anything different. Having a favourite chair is a bad routine.

Most wildlife fits in; to be an object of ridicule, like, say, the kākāpō and frigatebird, bodes ill for survival. Things that look scary fare better. Which means, I suppose, that humour extends across species, and enjoys the same kind of universality as fear, but in a finer register. It signals both vulnerability and discernment. One of my favourite novelists, Lisa Alther, expresses my feelings exactly: 'humourless people scare me.'

FINALLY, CRUSOE

I performed the usual ungainly transition from land to water, careful not to end up facing backwards (sometimes it's a choice between that and tipping up the boat). I crossed to the fourth and final island, the biggest, maybe 200 metres in length, which was wooded enough to be mysterious. It, too, had an ancient stone-slabbed jetty, partially submerged, metaphorically an ancient relic of Roman times or earlier, when sea levels were lower. Think of those statues in the Med, waiting for inquisitive, bubble-making divers. Partial submersion is a beautiful kind of ruination: burial at sea, yet not a complete burial as the submerged wall, statue or building is still there, visible from the surface if you look through the refractive illusion of clear water. There, and waiting in some sense for our demise, the end of our brief and aggressive tenancy of the land. All ancient things reproach us for ignoring their real lesson: the impossibility of making plans.

I landed and saw immediately some bedraggled detritus left behind by modern Swallows and Amazons. Split birch wood for a fire weighted down a soggy, olive green foam camping mat. Further up the slope, a big tarp covered more gear. These were not discarded things, they were waiting to be used again by someone rich enough to leave them behind. That's why I thought of a modern *Swallows and Amazons*: well-fed members of the bourgeoisie. Either that, or cross-over campers brought up on the crash-and-burn philosophy of festivals where tents and sleeping kit are routinely abandoned in the face of something no hangover relishes: packing.

I spent a while looking at the tarp, which was tied down in a way that meant: keep out. I assumed there was more camping gear under there – but what if it concealed a body?

I told myself it was my duty as a concerned and nosey citizen to make sure no corpse was under wraps. It is a common feeling I have had since childhood: that bodies wrapped in plastic are liberally scattered over the country-side, usually in semi-urban waste ground, corners of parks or liminal zones such as the island I was now on. I never think of finding a body on top of airy Ben Nevis or Ilkley Moor. In my mind, the location must reek of conspiracy and attempted concealment; for me, the edgelands are essentially body disposal sites, the necessary flipside of suburbia, where death has been airbrushed out of the picture.

I lifted up the tarp, wondering what I would do *if* there *was* a body. Would I drop everything and paddle furiously into Grasmere to raise the alarm? Or would I poke around to 'make sure' the dead body was actually dead? Once, on a walk along the South Downs, I saw a man lying face down but apparently stark naked, with his buttocks visible above the medium length grass. He looked dead, so I said loudly,

'Er, are you dead?' There was no response. To hell with it, I thought, if he's dead there's nothing I can do about it, and I walked on still feeling guilty. But this time, the flipped-back tarpaulin, after dumping its leafy load of rainwater, revealed only a few saturated and rolled-up sleeping bags and foam mats.

Nearby, another stone-ringed fireplace. The pine-needly path rose up and then down past rhododendron trees. These were too sparse for 'rhodie bashing', running over the tops of such bushes and diving into them, which others told me was perfectly possible though I had never done it myself. The tip of the island was dense with foliage and the feeling of going downhill and at the same time being slowly constricted into an isthmus or narrowing salient made for a claustrophobic feeling; I almost turned back. But something drove me on, if not the now compulsive feeling that I must explore or at least walk the main dimensions of each island.

Ahead, I saw a stone that at first I took for a menhir of some kind but then quickly realised it was the back of a grave. I'd been right, bodies were buried here.

It was a regular Victorian gravestone and on it was inscribed:

In MEMORY OF CRUSOE
a noble Newfoundland Dog
who for twelve years was the faithful follower of his owner
A J H le FLEMING
Born at Weston Super Mare
SEPT 1859

Died at Rydal Hall*
OCT 1st 1871

It was a very respectable gravestone. And a wonderful place
to be laid to rest.

---

* No longer the ancestral home of the le Fleming family, Rydal Hall is now
a conference centre.

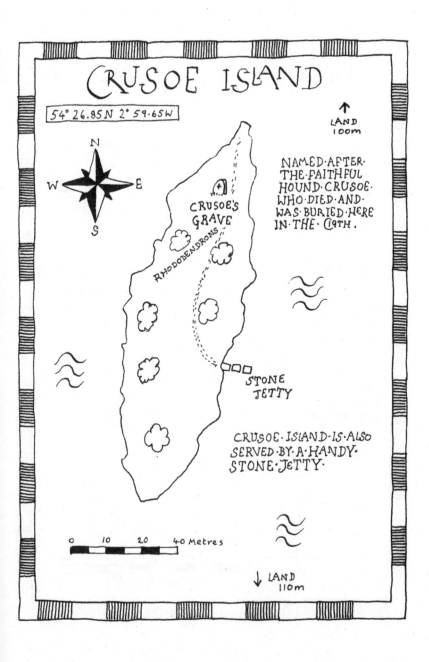

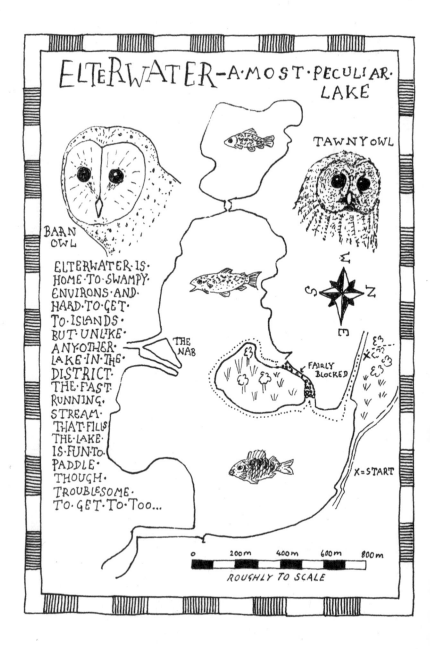

ELTERWATER - A·MOST·PECULIAR·LAKE

BARN OWL

TAWNY OWL

ELTERWATER·IS· HOME·TO·SWAMPY· ENVIRONS·AND· HARD·TO·GET· TO·ISLANDS· BUT·UNLIKE· ANY·OTHER· LAKE·IN·THE· DISTRICT· THE·FAST· RUNNING· STREAM· THAT·FILLS· THE·LAKE· IS·FUN·TO· PADDLE· THOUGH· TROUBLESOME· TO·GET·TO·TOO...

THE NAB

FAIRLY BLOCKED

X=START

0   200m   400m   600m   800m

ROUGHLY TO SCALE

THIRTEEN

Swamp Fever

Lake: Elterwater, 6.1 metres deep, 1.18 kilometres long, 0.28 square kilometres
Island: Dogowood Island

Another bad night in the car, perched on the side of the road; off the road, but not off it enough to avoid the floodlit outrage of passing cars. Why didn't I stay at an Airbnb like everyone else? It was partly a desire to have nothing to do with the internet or my phone while I was up here and partly a very real belief that 'the fork' required me to take ludicrous and uncomfortable choices from time to time to ward off the complacent comfiness of 'earth sickness'. Earth sickness is a very real disease that affects the well-off who also happen to be healthy, happy and successful. As if life wasn't devious enough already? These utterly charming, usually kind and helpful and well-heeled folk spend their lives enjoying the best the planet has to offer: top Michelin nosh, great hotels, foreign holidays to die for, art exhibitions and wonderful brunches with their adorable children and grandchildren. Yet behind their utter intoxication with how great everything is on this planet is a nagging feeling that they have missed something, some crucial piece of the puzzle; I mean they have all the rest . . .

Not much chance of me getting infected with that particular ailment . . . but you never know, so the car's increasingly damp interior is my home again for the long hours of night. The rolled-up canoe oozes water into the front seat, it's like sharing the car with a dead seal. I have another fairly crap thriller to read by the light of my head torch; thankfully the book is mercifully long. I am also pleased the book is not too good: if it was I'd be forced to stay up reading. I need the narcotic effect of a book, and the longer the better, rather than it being excitatory. I'm sure publishers are aware of this market for slightly boring books – after all, there are enough of them out there – and I found this one for free at Didcot Parkway train station.

Elterwater is more popular than you might think. It's not a famous lake and it doesn't look very inspiring from the road. But it has good parking and can be reached by a pushchair-friendly, smooth gravel path that allows half a lakeside circuit, with views of a sort and places to feed the ducks. Who would have thought, then, that this would turn out to be the wildest lake with the best stowaway possibilities of all?

It has a good stock of fish too, including the introduced wels catfish, a wide-mouthed predator that can live for fifty years. Its name comes from the same root as 'whale' and like a mini whale, it inhales fish whole into its mouth. It is unusually sensitive to smell and can hunt at night. In Europe, from where it was introduced, specimens have been known to reach 3 metres in length and over 450 pounds in weight. The largest caught in the UK weighed 147 pounds.

In Elterwater they rarely get bigger than 22 pounds and a metre long. Which is still pretty huge.

Judging by the map, the island (and I thought there might be more than one) appeared to be at the opposite end to that visited by tourists. This was the wilder, swampier, hard-to-get-to end. I pondered just how to achieve this for a while, and made a false start across a field that obviously belonged to a house with people inside. I went up the road instead and then across more agricultural-looking fields, which necessitated a high-stepping traverse of barbed wire. As I landed, all muddy and be-rucksacked, on the fine white gravel, pushchair-friendly path that led to the lake, I met a double family expedition of small kids and parents. It felt like I had just gate-crashed a pleasant children's outing or party, the kind of party I didn't mind *that much* when I had to take my own kids to them, but by golly I was glad that phase of fatherhood was over. The sheer madness of waiting on kids rather than have kids wait on us!* The day had started late and I was aware that the light would be fading soon. According to the compass, the river that fed the lake should have been dead ahead, but it wasn't. All the time I was dithering on the gravel, one of the kids was watching me with an exceptionally large pump-action water gun, presumably empty as he didn't fire at me, but if he did . . . I needed to find my way to the lake quick.

Since I could not find such a path, I simply got out of the range of parents and their water gun-wielding kids and blundered my way through swampy forest along indistinct animal trails, the kind that almost look like a proper path

---

* Sarcasm, maybe ironic too.

except they peter out for no apparent reason after going over a log or past a tree. A few strands of deer hair on a thorn bush, a hoof print in the mud tell you this is not a path for humans.

This forest reminded of the half-wild woodland around Jarn Mound, my place of adventure from the age of eleven onwards. Birch, swamp willow, dogwood and damp, straw-like grass. If you couldn't find a path you could make one, at a certain cost, a certain level of entanglement. The thing was, you could more or less see where you were going, until you were lost. It was woodland of just that kind of density, enough visibility to encourage off-piste exploration but not enough to allow safe transit without losing your bearings. Murkwood.

I pushed through the drippy birches, which were not that high. There was no sense of a high canopy. It was a low but extensive wood. The trees were willows and birches with wet patches in between. The birch was the first tree to colonise Britain after the great ice sheets retreated. It's always been a pioneer tree, relatively short-lived, few are over a hundred years old. Birch is called *bjørk* in Norwegian, which must be quite fun to say. Its bark is like lighter fuel and will outlast the easily rotting wood within for many years.

Pushing through the trees, I came at last upon a fast-flow-ing river that entered the lake. I could just about glimpse the lake away downstream, a fast, muscular stream coming from the darkness of the wood and bulging its way out into the demure lake with its pushchair-friendly, circumambulat-ing path. The feeling of contrast was not unsettling, it was defining part of the kind of wilderness I was almost most at home in, the kind I'd grown up with: edgelands, patches of wilderness right next to manicured, machine-friendly living spaces.

Though a lot has been written about edgelands, there is a sense in which they are inevitable once you desire or require a certain level of faux nature to disguise the ugliness and ambition of much urbanisation. Edgelands are the dark side of suburbia. Once you desire the simulacra of space, grass and trees, you create the spaces in between, those that are necessarily fallow owing to building regulations, plot sizes and communication requirements. All the elements of suburbia, which are naturally far more contradictory than those of a pure urban space such as Soho or Montmartre, and which are under a great tension to pull apart, explode, are held like a culture in aspic by the wild integuments that spring from untended soil, closed-off back lots and marshy riverside woodland such as the one I was now pressing on through.

It seems no surprise that the homeless increasingly reject the concrete uncertainties of the city for the nostalgia of an edgeland existence. In the town of Bridport where I used to live, the homeless favoured a triangle of land under a mobile phone aerial – a dry ditch that ran between fields used for public events and a dog walkers' copse that decorated the slopes of a reservoir hill overlooking the town. The mobile phone encampment struck me as both peculiarly crafty yet sacrificial at the same time. As if to emphasise this, a bolt of lightning struck the beautiful Scots pine tree next to the aerial and burnt it to a black relic. (Oddly enough, there had been a campaign waged by the town against the mobile company, who wanted to chop this tree down, or at least seriously pollard it. After the lightning strike, the company did just that to the other two pines, and so, from being a wonderful clump of trees hiding the skeletal ladder and dishes of a phone tower, it became a triumph of angular steel over stunted, hacked-back nature.) Not long afterwards, the phone company took possession of the space under the tower and strimmed it clear, making a hidden tent impossible. For several years prior to this, the homeless had banked on no one telling on them and since the company never or very rarely visited the site, they had been free to hide away there. But the essential element had been the phone company's initial desire to 'fit in' to the natural landscape – which they were happy to do until their authority was being thwarted and then, of course, the metal gloves came on. The homeless moved on, betting their freedom on the interstices provided by the sluggish response times of 'The Man'.

I followed the river and without warning went up to my waist in a sudden deep bog. It was a shock, but I was wearing my waders so I felt only foolish rather than wet and foolish. I quickly hauled myself out, using a small birch tree, reassured by the fact that the incident caused a broadly humorous kind of feeling, cheerfully told off, while also making me a bit more careful.

I broke out the packraft and inflated it quickly, grateful yet again for the ingenious airbag inflation method – the kind of thinking only a small newly formed company, eager to do their best, would come out with. Now most packraft companies have copied the same device, but they would have stuck to pumps if there had not been this example. In fact, packrafting, which is only slightly different from inflatable kayaking (yet this slight difference makes all the difference, like the difference between a mountain bike and a road bike), could never have happened without the high standards of the early companies, who, nevertheless, now overcharge for their product. Such are the contradictions of capitalism . . .

I put into the fast river, wondering as always if I'd be swept away. But of course the river is never as fast as it looks, and once you're moving in it you have enough time to think, to act. The trees leant over the water like corbelled arches; dark branches on both sides of the river curved overhead, hemming in the experience. On the far bank, there was more dense marshy woodland, more dripping birches and willows, and then darkness and the strangeness of swamps, which kept out everyone.

I allowed myself to be swept along towards the light, the opening out into the lake. Even there, the light was falling; there was maybe an hour and a half left before nightfall. It was gloom-laden and spitting with rain and it felt like an adventure already.

After a few guiding paddle strokes, I was midstream and shifting fast towards the bland touristic lake, which, to be honest, would not be out of place in somewhere like Rickmansworth or Cheam; except this is England, where topography changes in a few yards: up a bit and somewhere around to the west, I could already glimpse the outline of the mysterious hidden mangrove swamp island of Elterwater, which I decided to call Dogowood Island.* I paddled into the lake. On the far side, the last of the families were leaving. I ignored them to concentrate on working my way round the western edge of the still water that faced the swamplands with its drooping stunted trees and mysterious water

---

* D.O.G.O.: Dance Or Get Out.

channels. I went up one channel for five metres or fewer and it fractalised out into tens of smaller channels, and each one into ten more: a capillary system of water simultaneously irrigating and draining the wetlands. These channels ultimately connected to those on the other side of the swamp, cutting off a section – which was indeed the island I sought. Here, I saw my first and only piece of litter on Elterwater: a punctured kids' football lolling in a backwater, green with weed below the waterline. The general absence of litter gave me hope, for it signalled the absence of people who had come before me.

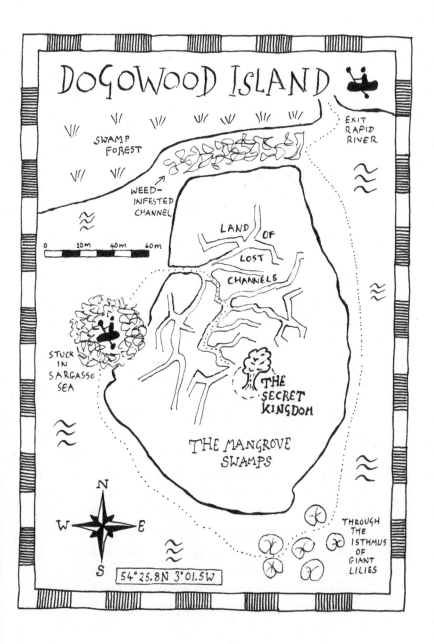

Back on the lake, I knew I needed a more substantial inroad to explore or at least identify the perimeter of Dogowood Island. The lake began to narrow and underneath my fragile craft and all around me were spreading the sub-surface leaves of lilies. Green hands that did not impede my progress because my boat was so light; I liked passing over these lily fronds, which softly sounded and moved in slow motion as I passed, another living element to the voyage. Indeed, it was as if they were encouraging me in my progress in a mythological sense, given the somewhat merged identity of the lotus and lily, symbolising another gateway I had to pass through. I felt I was in an Indian tank or sacred pond, manoeuvring ever so slowly towards some incense-burning temple carved from ancient, defaced limestone out of the ghats. The faces of the lilies were the faces of drowned souls or water nymphs fleetingly entombed in the wet slithery leaves.

Twice I went astray and followed a clear cut of water, a lead, through floating bushes and weeds. I ended up dead-ending, not through lack of water but through the narrowing of the way between sprigly treelets and damp boughs. Once, I squeezed Bertha through the narrowest of gaps, the fork in a sodden birch tree, only to be forced back by a barrage of waterlogged timber and thorny bushes. Wet leaves and brambly bits snagging my Buffalo top, I back-paddled and searched for new ways to connect round to the river and thought I saw a way. Further and further I went into the dark interior of the mangrove swamp (technically

salt-loving trees but you get the picture of trees growing
in water), looking for a way out and also for dry land on
which to explore. I kept making quick decisions about the
route, rather in the way you have to quickly decide the way
when going down rapids. When I looked over my shoulder
I seriously doubted if I could remember the way I came in.
I should have marked my twists and turns with string like
Theseus in the labyrinth.

And up ahead there was some sort of land, dimly
glimpsed, right at the very heart of the island. Enough land
perhaps to make a hidden camp, far from any prying or
preying eyes, a place to hold out at the very margin of the
liveable world, but my way in the boat was barred; I would
have to wade and some of the gaps between roots were very
deep. With a narrower boat, hard-shelled to guard against
punctures, I could have kept going . . . maybe. I gave up my
quest but not before knowing that here, at last, I had found
the ultimate bug-out destination in the Lake District. An
island no one really knew about, had ever been to, nor would
be going to in the near future. A place completely secure and
hidden and fairly near (a mile, say) to top grade . . . parking.

I had grown accustomed to the gloom within the swamp,
but now I saw that it was actually getting dark everywhere.
Being lost here all night was not an inviting idea: I had to get
back before it was dark. But paddling out of the swamp was
easier said than done. I went a little too quickly up a water
path quickly chosen and found my way barred by branches.
I then had to think carefully: was this *really* the way I had
come? At the prospect of being stuck at night in this gloomy
place, the slight edge of panic appeared – which, if managed,
can mean pleasurable relief later on. I deliberately slowed

down, took it easy. I went down one blind alley after another, not really getting closer till I punched my way through a garden of light green weed and out onto open water.

I had escaped, but night was falling. Paddling in falling light has its own pleasures, as I'd discovered on Crummock Water. You begin to realise that the lake is a giant reflector and that it is the last place where the light dies; it is a generous place to be caught out in. I stopped to dawdle a bit. The rainy weather had gone. The sun was far below the horizon. Clouds rimmed with its last rays took on the hyperreal quality of things lit differently; the calm acreage of sky between was disturbed not a whit by things down here; up there, in the jet stream, it was Arctic stillness, a colossal blueness fading towards the surface tension curve of the horizon.

The last problem was where to get out. I could continue a long way to the tourist path or try to fight my way against the current, back up the river to where I put in. It was a blisteringly fraught contest of splashing and driving paddles, in which a moment's respite saw me dragged backward by the current. By sneaking up the far bank I avoided the main power of it. Then I zipped across to land and deflate the raft. But even here, in the marshy reeds, I put a foot wrong when getting out of Bertha and sank again up to my thigh in the marsh. It put me in a good mood again: this place protected itself from incomers.

Elterwater at first seemed rather a forlorn and uninviting place, definitely in the B team if not the C team of lakes. But all this was just camouflage. In terms of real wilderness, it was right up there, and I knew the surge of energy and good feeling I had came from the wilderness drug it supplied. The wilderness drug is really a rare form of nutrition that is essential to humans. You find it only in wild places, lonesome places; it's one gauge of a lack of being visited. That's why you can be fed by the wilderness drug at the centre of Chesil beach, which, though near to tourist sites and the town of Weymouth, is separated from the road by a long stretch of water, effectively cutting it off from any visitor not prepared to hike five miles along a noisy, sloping, pebbly beach. And I realised again that is where the nutrition lies – in real wilderness, in places where few people go.* We cultivate and manicure our national parks to make them user-friendly. Put in paths and roads and access points. But what we really need are fewer of these things. Look at the popularity of urban exploration – of visiting buildings and tunnels long locked up, places now devoid of human traffic. And this is what we want of an island: a place where we are the very first, a new beginning, a new planet.

---

* However, Britain should congratulate itself on being far ahead of some countries where footpaths through mountainous forest are actually paved.

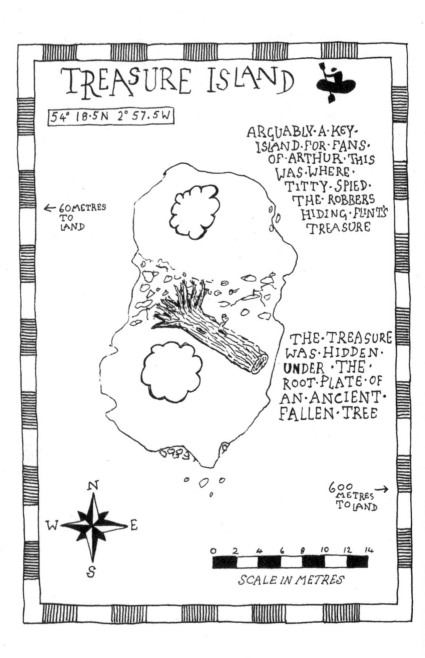

TREASURE ISLAND

54° 18.5N 2° 57.5W

ARGUABLY·A·KEY·
ISLAND·FOR·FANS·
OF·ARTHUR·THIS
WAS·WHERE·
TITTY·SPIED·
THE·ROBBERS
HIDING·FLINT'S
TREASURE

← 60 METRES
TO
LAND

THE·TREASURE
WAS·HIDDEN·
UNDER·THE·
ROOT·PLATE·OF
AN·ANCIENT·
FALLEN·TREE

600
METRES →
TO LAND

N
W   E
S

0 2 4 6 8 10 12 14

SCALE IN METRES

FOURTEEN

Treasure Island

Lake: Windermere (again)
Islands: Silver Holme, Blake Holme

Arthur Ransome played games with people who tried to nail him down over where was where in the Lake District with regard to his books. At the beginning and the end, he usually credited Peel Island with being Wild Cat Island, but then at other times he claimed Blake Holme was Wild Cat Island and that he had imported the Secret Harbour from Peel Island. This was supported by the fact that Silver Holme, on which Cormorant Island was based, stood in a similar relation to Blake Holme as Cormorant Island did to Wild Cat Island. And Cormorant Island is *the* treasure island in *Swallows and Amazons* even if the treasure is simply . . . Captain Flint's typewriter and the manuscript he had been writing all summer. Exactly: in a bit of self-reference that would have pleased Martin Amis, the typescript of *Swallows and Amazons* was saved by Titty (always suspected to be Ransome's favourite, now confirmed), since Flint represented aspects of Ransome, as we have already discovered.

But Blake Holme was much closer to the shore (almost

wadable) than the fictional Wild Cat Island was, though it was larger than Peel Island and had more obvious room for hiding a campsite. Also, the lookout point on Peel Island was arguably at the wrong end of the island and not as high up as Blake Holme. All these points needed to be answered before my journey could be concluded, and though it was pouring, deluging, with rain, it was to Windermere I returned to tie up the last pieces of my exploring.

I had spent the night, needless to say, sheltering in a former quarry, now a carpark, in hurricane-force winds. I was the lone inhabitant of said carpark and the wind was so high I moved the car to be out of the way if a tree fell. They were all swaying madly against the cloudy, blue-black night sky; getting out of the car was like going on deck on a cross-Channel ferry, the wind fair ripping your breath away. I woke early to pouring, driving rain, the kind that bubbles up like giants' tears as soon as the wiper blade has scraped the screen clear; the kind of super-abundant rain that makes you wish you had a faster windscreen wiper speed – making you forget that your usual thought is that the top wiper speed is *too fast*. Sometimes I even crouched forward to see more easily – a posture I'd always associated with my dad when huge lorries would routinely overtake our car on the M6, drenching it with hard-hitting spray and blinding our little Escort estate for a good few seconds; a charged and almost nightmarish start to any holiday north of the border.*

I drove down the unpopulated lower western side of

---

* Though my dad later became quite the motorway speeder, he was gripped in the 1970s (possibly as a result of the fuel crisis) by the urge to maximise mpg by driving at exactly 56mph at all times. Lorries calibrated to 60mph saw us as road prey.

Windermere that goes through woods and then alongside the lake and back into woods again. Finding a roadside lay-by, I sat for a while hoping the rain would stop. No chance. Wearing a Packa (a kind of poncho waterproof that covers the rucksack too), I headed into the woods to find the path that ran along the edge of the lake. I was almost exactly at the place where we had camped on my first trip to the Lakes when I was fourteen. In fact, we had probably seen some of the islands, maybe even Silver Holme, along the edge of the lake when we had gone exploring in our big orange Scout kayaks. But they had not been visited by me nor made any great impression on me then, at a time when I had passed from reading Arthur Ransome to Alistair MacLean, exchanging tales of boating for *The Guns of Navarone.*

The path along the lakeside was slick with wet leaves and wet root cables, mud and stones. It was up and down and across the occasional engorged stream blowing out from the land and into the silty-looking lake water, sprinkle patterned with pinpricks (or needle shafts, more like) of rain, an ordered quincunx spreading out into the rain-misty beyond; Blake Holme on the other side not even visible.

Silver Holme, though, was on this side. I planned to go there first and then cross the lake, if possible, and approach rain-sodden Blake Holme from a hidden side. The reason was the proximity to Tower Campsite, with its chalets and cabins and caravans, which was only metres away from the island on the far shore. That would simply not be right; I needed to block them from view, create my own fantasy reading of the place, a fantasy of a fantasy . . .

But where was Silver Holme? The path ran alongside a

sheep fence and a field and a sort of stately home or at least grand house. And then I saw the island, which stood in relation to the house as if owned by it, which was not what I wanted to see. A thick, fast, flooded stream broke under the fence and down to the lake – and right at its end was a spot hidden by trees where I could inflate the packraft and prepare for my last epic voyage. Not that anyone else was out in that weather.

Wiping drips from my nose and glasses, I got the boat inflated using the nylon inflation bag, doubly grateful in the rain for its rapidity and ease. The packraft bobbed and jiggled in the fast-flowing stream. But by now I knew its capabilities and I wasn't as nervous as I once had been. I got in and was carried with stately momentum towards the island. Which was only about seventy metres away, maybe fewer.

So, finally at Titty's island. And perhaps it is finally time to expatiate upon her embarrassing name (after that of Roger the cabin boy, of course). That Ransome had never come across the word 'tit' until he was an adult is quite likely. In literature, tit would mean a small bird or perhaps a titmouse. And even if he learnt the word's modern usage,* such late additions to one's vocabulary never have the emotional charge of words known from an early age. The middle classes were notoriously ill-educated when it came to vulgarities. When Mosley stood in Notting Hill in 1958, he famously

---

* Actually, the word 'tit' derives from 'teat', which comes from the old English *titt*. The term 'titty' was a nursery version of 'teat' that first appeared in the eighteenth century. On that note, we called my grand-mother 'Bubby', which was also a nursery term for breast that no one in my family seemed to know . . .

refused to change a poster featuring his head and the caption 'he is coming'. I have a friend called Richard Head who told me 'dick' simply wasn't a rude word when he was born in the 1960s.

In the 2016 film version of *Swallows and Amazons*, Titty is ludicrously renamed as Tatty. The thing is, I grew up knowing full well that Titty sounded a bit funny, but I chose to ignore the fact. I was able to make an imaginative leap to an earlier and, I imagined, a purer time. Just as I was able to convert the pounds, shillings and pence in Enid Blyton books into new money without the help of some moronic editor who 'updated' Blyton's works. There are very few things I absolutely loathe without rhyme or reason, but one of them is bowdlerisation. If you want a new version write something new: don't desecrate a sacred text.

Titty's island, where she hides out to escape the Amazon attack on Wild Cat Island and in the process overhears the burglars who use the place to bury Captain Flint's stolen trunk, is a key place in the book. It's where the dreamy Titty finally becomes a hero in contrast to the more robust Nancy and John and the more workaday but competent Peggy and Susan. Ransome is really Titty when it comes to dreaming, and dreaming is what he does best too.

It was a small wet island about thirty metres long. Lots of flat, mossy rocks and more vegetation than in Ransome's day. No cormorants. Some fallen pine trees and the remains (I thought) of the vast, fallen tree that dated from the 1930s and is mentioned in *Swallows and Amazons* as well as in Christina Hardyment's book *Arthur Ransome and Captain Flint's Trunk*.

BLAKE'S HEAVEN

But now I had to leave and make the final long voyage, the final journey to the last island of all: Blake Holme.

I was not looking forward to what would be my longest crossing in foul weather in the petite packraft (in the narrowed vision enforced by driving rain, Bertha had returned to being 'the packraft'). I did not have the heavy rucksack that had hampered my progress on Coniston; however, the water was much rougher and the wind higher. But despite the foggy rain, it wasn't *that* windy and Derwent Water had been much rougher.

I hastily set a course using the compass, as I couldn't even see where the island I was heading for was. The wind, coming from the south-west, more or less, blew directly into my face, and into the bulbous nose of the raft. It was quite clear to me that I faced a long and unpleasant journey but it all added to the experience of going to the last island.

From a distance, I suddenly made out its shape against the similar trees of the shore. Bigger than Peel Island, about 150 metres by 70, or so. Getting closer, I see that though this is a comely island it cannot be Wild Cat Island, because it lacks the harbour and the beach – and it is the landing places that really define an island. How you get onto the place is always important. Many islands are left alone because they are just too surf-splashed and rocky to access easily. Having its Secret Harbour as well as a handy beach to land on are what make Peel Island so enjoyable to visit, or at least form a big part of the reason. Blake Holme, like most of the Windermere islands, simply has rocky inshore waters beneath the spreading branches of trees extending over the lake; though at the southern end, if you avoid the rocks, there is a shingle beach and a nearby camp spot. You can land, and easily in a packraft, though it is immediately obvious how close you are to the lakeside. Even in Ransome's day the gap was closing and he cautioned in a letter that it was no longer safe to sail between the island and the shore. No Shark Bay, then. In the centre of the island were two fireplaces and a clearing – enough room for tents and places you could hide if someone was coming. It was the typical end to a journey – rather flat, miserable and wet, not a place to hang about.

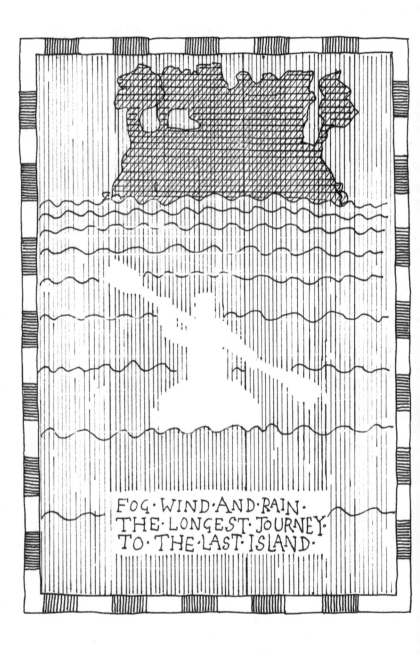

FOG · WIND · AND · RAIN ·
THE · LONGEST · JOURNEY ·
TO · THE · LAST · ISLAND ·

Rain lashed down harder; I had to return. With the wind almost behind me, it was a lot easier. From time to time rollers crept up and picked up the rear of the packraft and I almost surfed down waves. I kept checking over my shoulder for any double- or treble-sized waves, as I reminded myself yet again it is these anomalies that cause lake capsizes and I had no intention of emulating poor Ted Scott on Windermere almost a century before.

Ah, but there is cold, stung-faced satisfaction in breasting a stormy lake in driving weather, as inch by inch you claw your way closer to land. I headed south of Silver Holme to come in quite close to the YMCA lodge on that side of the lake. Drained and dripping, I rolled up the packraft for the last time on this trip and stuffed it in my saturated backpack. Then I got lost in the woods while trying to find the road, but by ignoring the map and following my nose I found it soon enough. Back in the car, I put the heater and blower on full blast and waited for the steam to clear.

A good enough place to pause and think of the all of it, the summing up, which on reflection is something like this: the lure of prolonging childhood in this new century is something to do with the infantilisation of self required to maintain sanity in the day-to-day dealings of the planet. If you can enjoy Disneyland rather than despise it, you'll have a nicer life . . . But I had glimpsed that all that was called 'adult' was not always good (just because you can draw an effective boundary between self and other doesn't make you, a priori, a good person) and in childlike adventures there lay a way of outwitting the infantile by *turning up* and *stepping up* . . .

My love of Arthur is tempered now by compassion. Like many of us, he couldn't and didn't always step up, but by golly he certainly turned up.

I started the car and ploughed through several deep puddles that extended right across the road. The road was running with water, both side gullies in flood, carrying bits of leaf and stick in the muddy water. At one puddle, a veritable flood in the hollow between two small hills, a cautious Lexus driver had pulled over to wait. I knew that it would only get worse and carried on through it, enjoying the churning splash around the doors. In a fulfilling combination of machismo and anxiety, derived from watching countless movies where cars sped through water, I felt rather superior to Lexus man since my low-slung Honda was definitely closer to the water than his. With a ferocious bubbling under the footwells and a sense of rising up, I surfaced onto slick tarmac, again having survived my baptism. Grateful for that, and reborn into something subtly different.

The world or my perception of it is always changed by a trip: something born from experience hatches out inside you, not always explainable. And to revisit the meandering idea that there is a fork in the path ahead in life, I would now artfully alter that image to one of a tuning fork, resonating, vibrating, making a single clear note – if you can only find a place quiet enough to hear it. The gross and simplified idea that you should take the path less grumpy, the way less tetchy and irritable, the track less self-centred, are not themselves the real message – but thinking about them, realising there is 'something in them', is. Because that moment when you pause and think about the direction of your way of living, that moment, that's when you can lean your head out of the car window, parked up, in some quiet spot and just listen. Who knows what might come back to you?

Fiddling with the radio now, I learnt that Keswick was cut off by floods and more roads were being closed all the time. It was a race against the deluge to leave the Lake District, a determined drive mediated by the wipers on full power (of course, not enough) and the need to stare intently to see the road ahead.

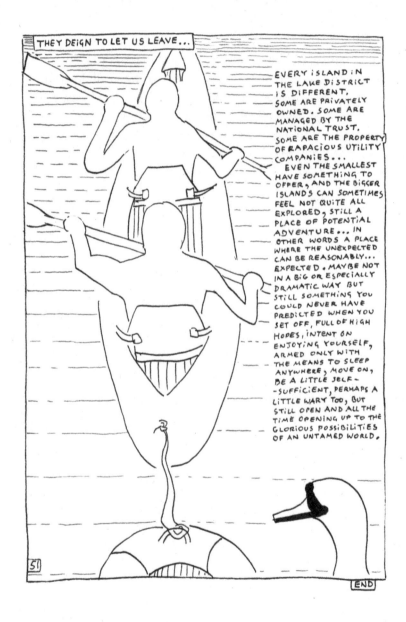

Afterword/Afterward

Have I said it all? Are there any loose ends to tie up? I recently read Victor Sebestyen's excellent biography *Lenin: The Man, the Dictator, and the Master of Terror* and Ransome seems a greater fool for *not* having discerned the utter brutality of the man. The evidence suggests that for sheer willingness to have people shot, Lenin outranked even Stalin. But of course a tolerance for tyranny is to be expected in men who never grow up: children are able to accept tyrants, play around at their feet, ignore the bigger picture as long as they receive plentiful and pleasant attention. And when you have your fill of the adult world, and knowing you have, in some way, missed what others see, you retreat to your own little island, another childish wish.

The survivalist's love of the apocalypse is not grounded in real notions; rather, the notion of the end plays second to the desire to escape, and it is the collapse of society that will set him or her free, free to be a child again, free to seek out a 'bug-out' spot, a place in the wilderness where at last he or she will be free from adult supervision.

When you write a book, it cures in some miraculous way any (well, most) hang-ups you might have about the subject you are dealing with. Harder work than therapy but much cheaper . . . In this book, I think I exhausted my desire for that secret spot, the perfect hide-out, the bolthole, the off-grid getaway. For better or for worse, we're all in this together.

My companion in stealth exploration, the packraft, is rolled up and put away. But the canoe is ready to use again. I am less bothered about taking the road well travelled now. I am even contemplating a trip down the busy Thames. In the commonest places you can find little half islands, half hidden from the mainstream, a small beach to land on, a place to pitch a tent and maybe make a fire – and that's all you need, however near and noisy the rest of the world is. It is your home.

The trouble with finding the extraordinary in the ordinary is that it doesn't get the pulses racing. It doesn't provide headlines. But think of those summer evenings spent playing on old wasteland, where the night was endless and the air alive with cicadas, and nothing you could say would alter the utter closeness of the stars, nothing you could say; and years later, at a chance meeting, you are reminded of the time you lay back and watched for meteorites, shooting stars dashing in miraculous short–long arcs, other worlds yielding their treasure constantly.

Acknowledgements

The completion of this book was vastly helped by a generous grant from the Royal Literary Fund; the award was guided through with wonderful speed and sympathy by Eileen Gunn. I thank them for their marvellous, non-bureaucratic work in supporting writers who have a track record of publishing worthwhile books.

In a random order I am indebted to many: Samia Hosny, the Estate of Arthur Ransome, Ella McCreath, Shaun Bythell, Jessica Fox, Stuart Kelly, Bijan Omrani, Christopher Ross, Mark Antcliff, Elizabeth Allen, Bill Coles, Lee Randall, Vivian French, Adrian Turpin, Lloyd Evans, Martyn White, Anthony Twigger, Jean Twigger. For the help my blog and newsletter have provided me with, see roberttwigger.com

Also by Robert Twigger

Walking the Great North Line
White Mountain: Real and Imagined Journeys
in the Himalayas
Angry White Pyjamas: An Oxford Poet Trains with
the Tokyo Riot Police
Big Snake: The Hunt for the World's Longest Python
The Extinction Club
Being a Man
Voyageur: Across the Rocky Mountains in a
Birchbark Canoe
Lost Oasis: A Desert Adventure
Real Men Eat Puffer Fish
Dr Ragab's Universal Language (a novel)
Red Nile: A Biography of the World's Greatest River